MEASURE FOR MEASURE

Text and Performance

GRAHAM NICHOLLS

M
MACMILLAN

© Graham Nicholls 1986

First published 1986

Published by
MACMILLAN EDUCATION LTD
Houndmills, Basingstoke, Hampshire RG21 2XS
and London
Companies and representatives
throughout the world

Typeset by
Wessex Typesetters
(Division of The Eastern Press Ltd)
Frome, Somerset

Printed in Hong Kong

British Library Cataloguing in Publication Data
Nicholls, Graham
Measure for measure: text and performance.
– (Text and performance)
1. Shakespeare, William. Measure for measure
I. Title   II. Series
822.3'3   PR2824
ISBN 0–333–34982–2

CONTENTS

Illustrations appear in Part Two

ACKNOWLEDGEMENTS

The text used in this study of *Measure for Measure* is that edited by J. M. Nosworthy for the New Penguin Shakespeare, published in 1969.

The author would like to thank the staff of the Birmingham Central Reference Library and the Nuffield Library, Shakespeare Centre, Stratford-upon-Avon, for their positive assistance in the writing of this book.

TO THE STAFF AND STUDENTS
OF
THE ENGLISH DEPARTMENT,
UNIVERSITY COLLEGE, SWANSEA,
1965–8

GENERAL EDITOR'S PREFACE

For many years a mutual suspicion existed between the theatre director and the literary critic of drama. Although in the first half of the century there were important exceptions, such was the rule. A radical change of attitude, however, has taken place over the last thirty years. Critics and directors now increasingly recognise the significance of each other's work and acknowledge their growing awareness of interdependence. Both interpret the same text, but do so according to their different situations and functions. Without the director, the designer and the actor, a play's existence is only partial. They revitalise the text with action, enabling the drama to live fully at each performance. The academic critic investigates the script to elucidate its textual problems, understand its conventions and discover how it operates. He may also propose his view of the work, expounding what he considers to be its significance.

Dramatic texts belong therefore to theatre and to literature. The aim of the 'Text and Performance' series is to achieve a fuller recognition of how both enhance our enjoyment of the play. Each volume follows the same basic pattern. Part One provides a critical introduction to the play under discussion, using the techniques and criteria of the literary critic in examining the manner in which the work operates through language, imagery and action. Part Two takes the enquiry further into the play's theatricality by focusing on selected productions of recent times so as to illustrate points of contrast and comparison in the interpretation of different directors and actors, and to demonstrate how the drama has worked on the modern stage. In this way the series seeks to provide a lively and informative introduction to major plays in their text and performance.

MICHAEL SCOTT

8

PLOT SYNOPSIS AND SOURCES

In order to enforce his neglected laws against sexual immorality, Vincentio, Duke of Vienna, announces his departure and his plan of handing over power to Angelo. The Duke remains in the city disguised as a friar to watch his deputy's behaviour. Angelo's regime opens with an attack on the brothels but the first victim of the capital law against fornication is Claudio, who has got Juliet with child. Claudio asks Lucio to inform his sister Isabella of his fate and asks her to plead with Angelo for his life. Isabella is on the point of entering a convent but she agrees to talk to Angelo. In pleading for her brother Isabella awakens Angelo's sexuality and at a second meeting he proposes that if Isabella will sleep with him he will pardon Claudio. Isabella rejects the suggestion but her brother begs her to accept Angelo's proposal. Isabella reproaches Claudio for his moral cowardice. The Duke meanwhile has been observing their meeting and suggests a counter-attack on Angelo. At an earlier period Angelo has jilted Mariana and she has gone into gloomy isolation. The Duke suggests that Isabella pretend to agree to Angelo's suggestion but that Mariana take her place in his bed. Mariana agrees to the plan but Angelo breaks his word and confirms the order for Claudio's execution. The Duke brings the Provost of the prison into his intrigue, who suggests that the head of a deceased prisoner be sent to Angelo. The Duke tells Isabella that her brother has been executed on Angelo's orders. The campaign against prostitution continues and Lucio gleefully paints for the Friar a slanderous picture of the 'absent' Duke's activities. Concealing his knowledge of Angelo's behaviour, the Duke returns in his own person to receive the accusations of Isabella. At first these are rejected and Lucio leads another slanderous attack on the Friar. When it is revealed that the Friar and Duke are the same person the Duke orders Angelo to marry Mariana, the ceremony to be followed by his execution. Mariana pleads for Angelo's life and Isabella joins in her appeal. But the Duke only pardons Angelo when Claudio is brought from the prison. In his final judgements Claudio is ordered to marry Juliet and, for slandering the Duke, Lucio is condemned to marry a prostitute. The Duke proposes marriage to Isabella.

SOURCES

Shakespeare's immediate sources are the two-part play by George Whetstone, *The Right Excellent and Famous Historye of Promos and Cassandra* (1578) and a story in the second part of Giraldi Cinthio's *Hecatommithi* (1565). Cinthio dramatised the story in his play *Epitia*. The ultimate source of the sexual proposition may be based on a true story. Other plot elements, such as the disguised ruler and the so-called 'bed trick', are found widely in world folk literature.

PART ONE: TEXT

1 INTRODUCTION: THE PROBLEM OF A 'PROBLEM' PLAY

In 1898 George Bernard Shaw observed that Shakespeare had made no attempt to 'pursue genuinely scientific method in his studies of character and society'. None of his plays could therefore be regarded as 'intellectually coherent drama'. From this blanket condemnation Shaw excluded *All's Well that Ends Well*, *Troilus and Cressida* and *Measure for Measure*. These were plays, Shaw conceded, which proved Shakespeare was 'ready and willing to start at the twentieth century if the seventeenth would only let him' (Preface to *Plays Unpleasant*). Two years earlier F. S. Boas had also grouped these plays and attached to them the term 'problem play'.

As applied to *Measure for Measure*, the term has developed what is perhaps an intentional ambiguity. In using an Ibsenite term the earlier critics implied that Shakespeare was rationally examining certain 'problems', especially those dealing with man's place in society, and sexual morality. But, as critical comment accumulated, the problem in *Measure for Measure* became the play itself. Some of the problems were particular and have always troubled critics: what are we to make of the Duke's behaviour, Isabella's defence of her chastity, the judgements of the finale? Other issues are more general: is the mood of the play bitter, realistic, satirical? Are we entitled to view *Measure for Measure* as a Christian play? What is Shakespeare saying about the relationship of law and morality? The New Penguin editor succinctly summarises the 'problem' of *Measure for Measure*: 'There exists no single agreed formulation of what the play actually does or how well it does it.'

Although Shakespeare wrote many plays which present complex problems, in none of them is there such a sense as in *Measure for Measure* that Shakespeare was setting out to create a

grey world of shifting values, of motives half understood and
reasons briefly glimpsed by audience and character, of
irreconcilable attitudes and non-comprehension between
characters. Faced with this shadowy world of ambiguities, a
critic might hesitate before committing himself to any sort of
interpretation, and although I have attempted a coherent
reading of the play in Part One I am also aware that other
visions of *Measure for Measure* are offered by the directors,
designers and actors considered in Part Two. Indeed, in a play
which presents the case against those who live their lives on
rigid, monolithic lines, it is less than appropriate to assess this
play from one inflexible viewpoint.

I am aware that in centring my thoughts on *Measure for
Measure* around the character of the Duke I have been
influenced by recent powerful performances of the role in the
theatre. In doing so I hope that I have acted within the critical
philosophy of the 'Text and Performance' series, for the
interdependence of a play's critical and stage history is not
something which has always been acknowledged. Certainly
with *Measure for Measure* scholarly attention has focused on
whichever of its three leading roles was most powerfully
presented at the time. Isabella's character and the 'chastity
problem' were lively issues in the nineteenth century when
memories of Sarah Siddons were vivid; in the first half of this
century, towering performances of Angelo by Charles Laughton
(Old Vic, 1933) and John Gielgud (Stratford, 1950) shifted
attention towards the deputy.

In the last 250 years *Measure for Measure*'s strength as an
acting play has always given it a toe-hold in the repertory even
when it threatened to disappear under a weight of moralistic
disapproval. But in the later part of the twentieth century it is
not merely a wish to see how actors tackle the parts of Angelo,
Mariana and Pompey which has given *Measure for Measure* its
boost in popularity. The play's complex treatment of complex
questions, its attack on moral absolutism, have meant that this
play is the easiest to ascribe to Shakespeare Our Contemporary.
Whatever we might think of Shaw's wish to see a rational spirit
at work in *Measure for Measure*, we would have to concede that
the twentieth century is now more than ready to accept this
play. It has in fact found its time. It is with the characters which

have prevented the play dropping out of the repertoire altogether that we begin our textual examination.

2 THE DUKE AND THE FRIAR: 'ONE THAT CONTENDED TO KNOW HIMSELF'

A useful starting-point for considering the Duke is to examine his relationship with the equivalent figures in Shakespeare's sources. The original story of the official and the condemned man's wife appears to be based on an incident from Italian history. The official proposes that the woman sleep with him and the man will be released. The official breaks his word, the man is executed and the widow appeals to the ruler of the country. The official is exposed, compelled to marry the woman, and executed. In the original story and in Shakespeare's immediate source, George Whetstone's play *Promos and Cassandra*, the king appears only as *deus ex machina*, listening to pleas for mercy and handing out justice with exemplary correct moral responses.

Shakespeare's principal adaptation to this flat figure is to draw on the folk theme of the disguised ruler, the man who learns about his realm by being treated like the man in the street, who checks up on the administration of justice at grass roots. Thus Shakespeare's Duke, in disguise as Friar, is sometimes observing, later intervening in, the action. This plot device could also carry comic implications, and Shakespeare had made serious and comic use of the theme in the scenes of *Henry V* on the night before Agincourt. In fact the disguised-ruler story carries some of the corrupt-judge plot, and, as in almost all versions of the former, the finale is taken up with the ruler drawing on his observations to hand out sentences on corrupt officials. This *dénouement* will be effective theatrical material as the ruler plays cat and mouse with his unsuspecting deputies.

The effect of combining these two traditional elements is to give us a character who is at once an observer, an intriguer, and a potential *deus ex machina*. For, despite the serious nature of what they are watching, an audience is led to believe that a man is on hand to set all to rights. It is also of the essence of the disguised-ruler story that the ruler learn about his realm either in observation of corruption or in a deeper understanding of how his subjects live. It will become apparent that the Duke of Vienna has a longer and more tortuous process of self-discovery. He will learn awkward truths about the administration of justice but it is unclear how far these lessons have gone home.

The other area of uncertainty to which Shakespeare deliberately draws attention through treatment of his sources is the question of the Duke's transfer of power. In the earliest accounts the corrupt judge is a provincial administrator with executive powers deputed to him by the king. Only in Shakespeare does the ruler hand over administration to a deputy and then disguise himself to watch the results of his action.

We are compelled to ask for what purpose Shakespeare introduces these changes. At the outset of the play we are confronted with the ambiguity which permeates so much of it. For what the Duke says of Angelo in the first scene seems simple commendation of his transparent honesty and selfless devotion:

> There is a kind of character in thy life
> That to th' observer doth thy history
> Fully unfold. Thyself and thy belongings
> Are not thine own so proper as to waste
> Thyself upon thy virtues, they on thee.   [I i 27–31]

In his second scene, with Friar Thomas, the deputy is still described as 'a man of stricture and firm abstinence' [I iii 12], but the Duke now notes too his coldness, a non-human streak:

> Lord Angelo is precise,
> Stands at a guard with envy, scarce confesses
> That his blood flows, or that his appetite
> Is more to bread than stone.   [I iii 50–3]

Angelo's earlier relations with Mariana also cast a shadow across his eulogies. The Mariana story of course is introduced later, when it becomes necessary for the Duke to have a dark

secret from Angelo's past. But an audience casting back to the
beginning of the play will ascribe some of the Duke's doubts
about his deputy to knowledge of Angelo's questionable
dealings with Mariana:

> Hence shall we see,
> If power change purpose, what our seemers be.   [53–4]

Looking back with our later knowledge of Angelo's character
the Duke's speeches about him become a warning and a
proposed model for attainment rather than a description of his
present virtuous state:

> Heaven doth with us as we with torches do,
> Not light them for themselves: for if our virtues
> Did not go forth of us, 'twere all alike
> As if we had them not.   [I i 32–5]

What at first appears uncomplicated praise is also a
presentation of high ideals at which to grasp.

There are other signs of uncertainty in the Duke at the outset.
His opening remarks to Escalus are oblique, sometimes
obscure, and he appears very anxious 'of government the
properties to unfold' to someone whom he admits knows more
of the subject than he does. Twice he demands of Escalus, a
respected elder statesman, his opinion of the delegation of
power, and recent Dukes have interpreted these signs of
agitation as insecurity in his proposed plan.

His instructions to Angelo on how to act in his absence are
direct and transparent –

> In our remove be thou at full ourself.
> Mortality and mercy in Vienna
> Live in thy tongue and heart   [43–5]

– but this forcefulness takes us to a central question about the
Duke's competence. We are surely entitled to ask why he
himself has done nothing to remedy a worsening situation in
Vienna and why he now feels it necessary to entrust this duty to
someone else. Many characters regard this remissness as a

fault, and some of them see the handing-over of the problem to a deputy as a dubious artifice. When the Duke tries to face up to this question with Friar Thomas he reveals his understanding of the importance of the anti-immorality laws of his city:

> We have strict statutes and most biting laws,
> The needful bits and curbs to headstrong weeds,
> Which for this fourteen years we have let slip;
> Even like an o'ergrown lion in a cave,
> That goes not out to prey.   [I iii 19–23]

There is certainly a well-articulated body of opinion in *Measure for Measure* which holds that the laws against immorality are pointless and ineffective, but the Duke maintains that these laws are necessary to restrain men's rampant sexuality. The law is a necessary restraint on sexual anarchy and the Duke condemns himself for failing to invoke the restraint. In a memorable image the lusty cavortings of animal-like sexuality are contrasted with the flabby apathy of the law, the hunting lion who grows fat in his den. As a result of his dereliction of duty the Duke pictures his city in the traditional turmoil of 'the world turned upside down':

>   our decrees,
> Dead to infliction, to themselves are dead,
> And liberty plucks justice by the nose;
> The baby beats the nurse, and quite athwart
> Goes all decorum.   [27–31]

Faced with this vivid image of a society he himself has created, one can only agree with Friar Thomas's gentle stricture:

>   It rested in your grace
> To unloose this tied-up justice when you pleased,
> And it in you more dreadful would have seemed
> Than in Lord Angelo.   [31–4]

The Duke is moved to a partial defence of his behaviour, but his account is casuistical: to imply that, as it was he who sanctioned sexual immorality by allowing the law to be mocked, someone else should now enforce the law, could easily be reversed into the criticism that, since the problem is of his own creation, he should not now expect someone else to do his dirty work. Vincentio has allowed evil to flourish outside his court, whence he never stirs:

> Most holy sir, none better knows than you
> How I have ever loved the life removed
> And held in idle price to haunt assemblies
> Where youth and cost a witless bravery keeps.   [7–10]

His behaviour is not merely an understandable wish to avoid large crowds; it is a deliberate withdrawal from contact with his city and its people, a withdrawal which he confesses to be linked with the corruption of Vienna.

Once in disguise he begins to explore the legal world for himself and encounters the people he has hitherto avoided in all their messy humanity. In two of *Measure for Measure*'s most memorable cameo parts he meets examples of his lethargy as ruler. The bumbling constable Elbow is the best his parish can come up with for the post, a situation which the practically-minded Escalus finds intolerable, sending Elbow away to collect a list of other possible candidates. There is also the long-term prisoner Barnadine, who has been awaiting execution for nine years. The disguised Duke expresses surprise that 'the absent Duke has not either delivered him to his liberty or executed him'. The Provost is forced to admit that his crime 'till now in the government of Lord Angelo came not to an undoubtful proof' [IV ii 129–35]. We note the contrast between the tardiness of the Duke's administration and the speed with which Angelo's new regime brought the matter to a conclusion.

We are thus presented in the Duke with an insecure authority figure aware that his rule has created a stagnant, corrupt Vienna, yet handing over the task of rectifying the situation to an authoritarian of whose moral fibre he has enough doubt to linger in disguise to watch the consequences of his transfer of power. Later we shall consider the Duke's progress towards a kind of understanding of the law and morality, and his partial attempts to apply what he has learnt. Duke Vincentio can be regarded as one of that group of

Shakespearean rulers who, like Prince Hal and King Lear, go on a journey of discovery into the nature of law. But, whereas Hal's education in *Henry IV* is an apprenticeship to kingship and Lear has the bitter task of unlearning a long life of egoism, the Duke's lessons in *Measure for Measure* are learnt whilst he is nominally in the seat of justice. And in this grey world of tragi-comedy we are finally left to ponder how effective are the lessons learnt in his disguised wanderings amongst the morally unregenerate of his city.

3   ANGELO AND ISABELLA: 'ANGELS ON THE OUTWARD SIDE'

In contrast to the mysteries and ambiguities of the Duke's behaviour, the characters of Angelo and Isabella seem transparent and single-minded. What is at issue is the nature of our response to these two highly-principled characters. Angelo in particular is created very largely by what other people say about him. The Duke's opening description is followed, as we have seen, by a less certain account, and there is doubt and incomprehension in many references to Angelo which set a distance between him and the more overtly fallible law-givers and law-breakers of *Measure for Measure*. After being twice asked his opinion of the transfer of power, Escalus takes up a note which is to be heard several times during the play:

> If any in Vienna be of worth
> To undergo such ample grace and honour,
> It is Lord Angelo.   [I i 22–4]

'If any' must convey a flicker of a possibility that nobody could really 'be of worth' to undertake this task. Even though Claudio never questions the justice of his death sentence, his comments on Angelo's behaviour again underline the strain between the man and his office:

> Whether it be the fault and glimpse of newness,
> Or whether that the body public be

> A horse whereon the governor doth ride,
> Who, newly in the seat, that it may know
> He can command, lets it straight feel the spur;
> Whether the tyranny be in his place,
> Or in his eminence that fills it up,
> I stagger in.   [I ii 157–64]

And in Lucio's comically exaggerated pictures of Angelo we realise that the rest of Vienna does not understand, or basically trust, the Angelos of this world; his coldness and detached application of justice have made him the butt of ribald speculation.

The uncertainty, the non-comprehension, the downright scepticism with which Vienna sees Angelo is, up to a point, proved correct. He is also the Angelo the audience is watching up to the point where Isabella starts to attract him: a public man, self-contained and remote, but getting down to his appointed task of sorting out the moral disorder which the Duke has created. Angelo comes before us as an efficient servant of justice:

> We must not make a scarecrow of the law,
> Setting it up to fear the birds of prey,
> And let it keep one shape, till custom make it
> Their perch and not their terror.   [II i 1–4]

The animal analogy reminds us of the Duke's strictures on his regime to Friar Thomas and this is the first of several tactful criticisms by Angelo of the Duke's laxness. But in his over-exalted picture of himself as the law's impartial administrator Angelo opens himself up to later ironical judgement:

>   rather tell me,
> When I, that censure him, do so offend,
> Let mine own judgement pattern out my death
> And nothing come in partial.   [28–31]

After this theoretical approach to the law Shakespeare shows us, in the opaque case which Elbow brings against Pompey, the law in its day-to-day untidiness. It is Escalus who has to take up the exploration of the intricacies of the case of Mrs Elbow and the dish of stewed prunes after Angelo's patience breaks and he leaves the court with the wish that all the participants should be whipped. Angelo's refusal to deal with the minutiae of petty cases is a striking example of the incompatibility of his legalistic frame of mind and the stalwart refusal of the everyday world to fit itself into that framework. Although we may sympathise with his lack of intense interest in the precise cost of Pompey's fruit dish, Angelo's exasperation at the mundane actualities of administering justice weakens our feeling that Vienna will be the better for his rule.

The two central confrontations with Isabella will be dealt with in section 5. When, having thrown aside the image of himself as the impersonal instrument of the law, Angelo triumphantly assumes his new role of tyrannical seducer, he rushes from the stage and is not seen again until just before the return of the Duke. Of his greatest act of cruelty – breaking his work and executing Claudio – and his third meeting with Isabella, we hear at second-hand. This striking piece of stage-craft might be expected to soften the effect of the villainy, but by reducing him to an off-stage presence it turns Angelo into a faceless lecher, fussily demonstrating to Isabella the secret way into his garden, or a fumbling tyrant uncharacteristically underlining his instruction for Claudio's execution. The Angelo we do *not* see between ii iv 170 and iv iv 1 is an impersonal figure drained of dignity; when we see him again he is a shadow, not only of the bright-eyed man eager to take a new broom to the Viennese brothels, but also of the exuberant ruler excitedly entering into his role of sexual tyrant. The sharp legalistic mind which fenced so effectively with Escalus and, at first, with Isabella now indulges in fearful self-pity, generalised exclamations of regret for his murder of Claudio. When he is finally confronted with his accusers, Angelo's only remaining lines are two short speeches demanding punishment. His relative silence represents the final collapse of the strong-willed authoritarian we saw at the outset of his regime. In demanding that the swift hand of the law deal with him, Angelo pleads for condemnation by his own form of law; the Duke's eclectic response is to give him over to domesticity with Mariana and the knowledge that his failings have been exposed before the gates of Vienna.

So what of Isabella, the force that shatters Angelo's complacent image of himself as the objective voice of justice? Isabella has of course aroused even more critical controversy than the Duke, much of it being centred on her highly-charged defence of chastity. There has never been unanimous support for Isabella's stance, and I have little doubt that Shakespeare's audience reacted in as confused and varied way as at any other time in the 380 years of *Measure for Measure*'s stage history. Let us simply consider Isabella for what she is, for what she says and does, and what is said about her.

We first hear of Isabella by report when her brother asks Lucio to beg his sister's assistance in pleading for his life:

> in her youth
> There is a prone and speechless dialect,
> Such as move men; beside, she hath prosperous art
> When she will play with reason and discourse,
> And well she can persuade. [I ii 181–5]

This portrait of Isabella as a consummate rhetorician hardly squares with the nervous novice we see in the next scene or in the earlier part of her interview with Angelo. Furthermore, Claudio's language is reminiscent of the silver-tongued seducer, a ludicrous image we may feel for a young girl about to enter the convent, but one which will become ironically vindicated when her words unwittingly excite Angelo.

Isabella's first words are perhaps the oddest Shakespeare gives to one of his heroines. Entering at the point of her assuming her novitiate with the austere Order of St Clare, our first impression is that Isabella is uneasy with the restrictions about to be imposed on her: 'And have you nuns no farther privileges?' We are quickly put right:

> I speak not as desiring more,
> But rather wishing a more strict restraint
> Upon the sisterhood, the votarists of Saint Clare. [I iv 1–5]

As Angelo wishes to hide himself in the presumed objectivity of the law, so Isabella tries to isolate herself from the world within the constrictions of the nunnery. And, as Angelo's abstract legalism was immediately thrown against the confusion of the Elbow and Pompey farrago, so now Isabella comes face to face with Lucio, the embodiment of worldly sensuality in the play. Lucio too separates Isabella from the general mass of humanity:

> I hold you as a thing enskied and sainted,
> By your renouncement an immortal spirit
> And to be talked with in sincerity,
> As with a saint.   [34–7]

Isabella is removed by her own choice from the grubby world of sexual commerce.

Lucio's appeal draws Isabella out from a place in which she could have lost herself in rigid discipline. She must now use her own resources in the tough, troublesome legal jungle of Angelo. Her first responses to Lucio and Angelo are uncertain, and only gradually does she rise to eloquent descriptions of the Christian doctrine of redemption. Trapped into accepting Angelo's sexual offer, Isabella can only rage impotently as her brother refuses to live up to her image of him as a heroic figure who will gladly go to the block rather than accept his sister's dishonour. When this illusion is shattered and Isabella turns on the brother she has been trying to save, the Duke intervenes and the counter-attack on Angelo begins. The Duke is able to channel Isabella's anger into constructive intrigue, and this anger is the motive force that carries her along with the Duke's plans.

When Mariana is also involved in the intrigue, Isabella shows a new enthusiasm for the plot: it is she who initiates Mariana into the details of the attack, and in her third (unseen) interview with Angelo she assumes a role of compliancy. As she describes the scene of the proposed assignation there is a definite sense of Isabella's new pleasure in adventure.

Both the Duke and Isabella play their assumed roles in the finale with confidence: the Duke as incredulous governor, Isabella as wronged virgin. Spurred on by the Duke's deception, Isabella tells lies about her relationship with

Angelo, and, by her being allowed to believe that Angelo has had Claudio beheaded, tension is created before the climactic moment when Isabella, justifying in action her earlier Christian rhetoric, kneels for her brother's judicial executioner. I shall consider the question of her reaction to the Duke's proposal of marriage later, but, however she reacts, her marriage is a final turning-away from the private, enclosed, sexless world of the nunnery to the public domestic world of the Duchess of Vienna.

Both Isabella and Angelo are self-contained, isolated figures who are transformed by their confrontation with one another. Angelo's shell of legalism is smashed and the resulting lack of a role and sense of identity leads to his collapse; Isabella is brought out of the narrow world of the convent and, with the help of the Duke, directs her cloistered virtues into a positive force in the everyday world.

4 THE SEXUAL UNDERWORLD: 'POOR FELLOWS THAT WOULD LIVE'

The law-givers we have considered are portrayed as fallible, confused, or potentially corruptible. Their moral opposition are the Viennese law-breakers who proffer sex as a commercial venture, and their customers. In the first group are Pompey, Mistress Overdone and the whores; in the second, Lucio, the gentlemen of II ii, Froth and, up to a point, Claudio.

Shakespeare's view of this section of society is balanced, humane and clear-sighted as to their virtues and short-comings. Pompey is neither a lovable rogue nor a brutal criminal, but a man attempting to make a living in the way he knows best, a way which happens to be morally and legally reprehensible. His famous plea, 'Truly, sir, I am a poor fellow that would live' [II i 212], is, after all, part of a court-room justification in order to escape whipping. The exchange between Escalus and Pompey puts the case fairly for both sides:

ESCALUS. Pompey, you are partly a bawd, Pompey, howsoever you

colour it in being a tapster, are you not? Come, tell me true. It
shall be the better for you.
POMPEY. Truly, sir, I am a poor fellow that would live.
ESCALUS. How would you live, Pompey? By being a bawd? What do
you think of the trade, Pompey? Is it a lawful trade?
POMPEY. If the law would allow it, sir.
ESCALUS. But the law will not allow it, Pompey; nor it shall not be
allowed in Vienna.   [II i 209–18]

Pompey wishes to be left alone to pursue a profession without
the inconvenience of moral considerations. Were it not for the
minor problem of its illegality he would be happy to continue in
a calling that would then be perfectly legal. On the other side
Escalus restates the legal position with a minimum of
pomposity and a measure of humorous detachment; whatever
anyone might personally think of the law, it is there to be
enforced and if Pompey transgresses again he will be severely
punished. The balance of the argument has been maintained.
The law-breaker is free to ignore or thumb his nose at the law;
the law-giver will enforce the law as it stands.

In this case, the law deals relatively lightly with its victim.
The other line of Angelo's moral attack is on sexual intercourse
outside marriage. As its only victim in *Measure for Measure*,
Claudio receives our full attention, the pathetic martyr of a law
which the majority of characters regard as absurd. But on
inspection Claudio seems an odd figure for a totally
sympathetic victim. His moment of greatest humanity is at the
point of greatest despair when he invokes the horrors of the
afterlife he is about to encounter. But earlier Shakespeare has
deliberately blurred some key areas of Claudio's character,
especially the nature of his relationship with Juliet. We first
hear of him from Mistress Overdone, Lucio and his
companions, with whom he seems closely associated.
Overdone regards him as the most valued member of the
group, and Lucio refers to him as a boon companion. We may
not regard Pompey's earthy description of Claudio's offence –
'Groping for trouts in a peculiar river' [I ii 89] – as totally
objective, but nothing we have heard from Claudio's friends
suggests that in their world sexual relations mean anything
more than animal coupling, unwanted babies, and venereal

disease. When Claudio appears, his demeanour under the humiliation of public shaming is dignified if somewhat embittered, but Lucio is surprised to hear his hedonistic companion speak in such sober terms: 'If I could speak so wisely under an arrest, I would send for certain of my creditors' [130–1]. Juliet's silence and the lack of any speech between her and Claudio is confusing, but neither here nor in prison nor at their final reconciliation does Claudio speak of or to Juliet, nor does he refer to the child she is about to bear him. Indeed Claudio's disgust at what he regards as the outcome of a lustful conjunction is violent and loathsome:

> As surfeit is the father of much fast,
> So every scope by the immoderate use
> Turns to restraint. Our natures do pursue,
> Like rats that ravin down their proper bane,
> A thirsty evil, and when we drink we die.   [I ii 125–9]

When he attempts a defence of his behaviour he makes matters worse. The intransigence of Juliet's relations may have prevented the formal legislation of his affair but given the nature of Claudio's world we may feel that her relations had cause to be cautious. Shakespeare prefers to smudge our response to a man to whom our sympathy would naturally turn.

If Claudio is on the edge of the sexual underworld, Lucio is central to it. Although described as a 'fantastick' in the Folio's *dramatis personae*, a term usually glossed as 'fop', Lucio is far from the empty-headed fashion-follower of Restoration comedy. He can be witty, intelligent and sensitive, as well as gross, tactless and cruel. In the conversations of I ii he is a sharper, more intelligent libertine than his companions, and when he hears of Claudio's arrest he seems genuinely upset. His commitment to fight for his friend's release arises both from his affection for Claudio and a realisation of the absurdity of the law.

With Isabella Lucio is at his most gallant and sensitive. When explaining the nature of Claudio's offence, his language becomes circumlocutory as he attempts to break the news in a

gentle and polite fashion. Amusingly it is the novice nun who
bluntly cuts through his periphrasis:

> LUCIO. Your brother and his lover have embraced.
>   As those that feed grow full, as blossoming time
>   That from the seedness the bare fallow brings
>   To teeming foison, even so her plenteous womb
>   Expresseth his full tilth and husbandry.
> ISABELLA. Someone with child by him? My cousin Juliet? [I iv 40–5]

Lucio's uncharacteristic mealy-mouthed language contrasts
sharply with the 'men's talk' of his previous appearance in the
play.

Lucio's behaviour in the early part of *Measure for Measure* is
based on generous motives; in the prison scenes we see his more
callous side. There are hints that it was on his information that
Overdone, Pompey and the whores were arrested, and his
baiting of Pompey who is being taken off to prison reveals the
harsher side of the nonchalant man-about-town. This incident
leads into the first of the two most comically effective scenes in
Measure for Measure: Lucio's slandering of the disguised Duke.

I see no evidence to suggest that what Lucio says about the
Duke – that he is lecherous or over-indulges in drink – has any
vestige of truth, but, as the Duke comes to realise, these
rumours are rife because of the remoteness and isolation of his
life as ruler. His laxness in enforcing the Viennese morality
laws has been interpreted by his citizens as a personal
endorsement for sexual license:

> Would the Duke that is absent have done this? Ere he would have
> hanged a man for the getting of a hundred bastards, he would have
> paid for the nursing a thousand. He had some feeling of the sport.
> He knew the service, and that instructed him to mercy. . . . The
> Duke yet would have dark deeds darkly answered. He would never
> bring them to light.   [III ii 110–14, 166–8]

A regime which has left Barnadine to rot in prison for nine years
has bred rumours such as Lucio puts out with relish. The Duke
had realised that his indolence had corrupted Vienna, but
amongst the unregenerate members of the city he discovers that

his culpability for moral disorder is more positive and more personal: 'the old fantastick Duke' has lurked in dark corners not, according to some of his down-to-earth citizens, because of his natural diffidence but in order to satisfy his rampant libido.

The disguised Duke learns from these reports about his relationship with his subjects, and his return to power and the final judgements are carried out under the full light of the public gaze. But the Duke is not kindly disposed to the man who has been the unwitting agent in this discovery, and all Lucio's attempts to intervene in the finale are waspishly slapped down. The Duke's curt remarks to Lucio are something more than a desire to keep order during the unravelling of the intrigue. The fact that his teasings have provoked such vindictive anger again makes us wonder how comprehensive is his new understanding of justice. His personal pique against Lucio contrasts with his lofty disdain for Angelo. As Johnson observes, 'Perhaps the Poet intended to show, what is too often seen, that men easily forgive wrongs which are not committed against themselves'.

5 THE TWO ENCOUNTERS: AN EXAMINATION OF II ii AND iv

The excitement of the two central scenes of confrontation between Isabella and Angelo arises out of the moral to and fro between characters for whose firm standards we have been well prepared. At first Isabella is fearful, self-doubting, easily led into blind-alley arguments which Angelo blocks with ease, but, as her confidence increases, her language and rhetoric become more committed and Angelo is thrown into moral confusion.

Isabella's opening speech has all the air of a carefully prepared set piece lacking persuasive conviction:

> There is a vice that most I do abhor,
> And most desire should meet the blow of justice,
> For which I would not plead, but that I must,
> For which I must not plead, but that I am
> At war 'twixt will and will not.   [II ii 29–33]

It is difficult to conceive of a more diffident approach to a plea
for mercy: Isabella's nervous antitheses and her disarming wish
to expose her uncertainties hold no interest for Angelo's sharp
barrister mind and he can in effect reply, 'so what?' ('Well: the
matter?') Isabella is no more successful when she tries to argue
that Angelo should merely condemn fornication and not the
fornicator, a specious argument which arouses Angelo to a
more expansive reply. His clipped question, 'Condemn the
fault, and not the actor of it?' has the sarcastic court-room
lawyer's ring and he easily answers the facetious restatement of
Isabella's argument:

> Why, every fault's condemned ere it be done.
> Mine were the very cipher of a function,
> To fine the faults whose fine stands in record,
> And let go by the actor.   [37–41]

Not for the first time in this scene we are reminded obliquely of
the Duke's regime, when crimes were 'let go by' by a man who
was 'the very cipher of a function'.

Isabella realises the inadequacy of her position; she is unable
to argue for something of which she does not approve. It is
when Angelo turns to the particularities of Claudio's case and
Isabella is directly confronted with the fact of her brother's
imminent fate that she pitches her appeal on a higher level than
her earlier, cooler remarks:

> Well, believe this,
> No ceremony that to great ones longs,
> Not the king's crown, nor the deputed sword,
> The marshal's truncheon, nor the judge's robe,
> Become them with one half so good a grace
> As mercy does.   [58–63]

Isabella piles up the physical symbols of authority in order to
dismiss them in comparison with the power of mercy. Her
increased confidence of language reflects her new confidence in
the strength of her moral position and Isabella can argue
Portia-like for mercy as the greatest attribute of a good judge
and ask Angelo to try and put himself into the situation of a

exually responsive young man. It is possible for Isabella to maintain these moral postures whilst still condemning her brother's sin.

Angelo now shows the first signs that he is personally involved and asks her to leave. Lucio, the sensualist, seems to understand that Isabella is getting through to Angelo: 'Ay, touch him; there's the vein' [70]. But Angelo has still not lost his critical faculties and in the face of what he chooses to regard as sophistry he retreats to an abstract restatement of his position. The fact that he, a potential sinner, condemns a sinner is irrelevant; it is the law, of which he is an impersonal instrument, that condemns Claudio. But the notion of Angelo as a sinner has been introduced and instinctively Isabella moves to break down his impersonality by inviting him to feel a sexual response like the condemnéd man.

Whilst the combatants spar on an abstract level, Angelo can continue to insist on the objectivity of the legal system, but as before, a return to the fact of her brother's execution ('He must die tomorrow' [82]) unsettles the drift of Isabella's argument and she pours out her most directly passionate appeal for his life: 'Tomorrow? O, that's sudden; spare him, spare him' [83]. Her vehemence momentarily deflects her into a concession to libertinism as she tries to make light of his offence:

> Who is it that hath died for this offence?
> There's many have committed it.   [88–9]

This minimising argument arouses Angelo's most impressive statement of policy and his closest approach to criticism of the absent Duke's indolence:

> The law hath not been dead, though it hath slept.
> Those many had not dared to do that evil
> If that the first did th'edict infringe
> Had answered for his deed. Now 'tis awake,
> Takes note of what is done, and like a prophet
> Looks in a glass that shows what future evils,
> Either now, or by remissness new, conceived,
> And so in progress to be hatched and born,
> Are now to have no successive degrees,
> But, ere they live, to end.   [90–9]

Claudio must die in effect because of the Duke's laxness in enforcing the city's laws.

This direct application of legal theory to her brother's case launches Isabella into her greatest efforts, and in one of the most celebrated speeches in the play she contrasts the flexibility of heaven's response to justice with man's stiff application of the law:

> Merciful heaven,
> Thou rather with thy sharp and sulphurous bolt
> Splits the unwedgeable and gnarlèd oak
> Than the soft myrtle; but man, proud man,
> Dressed in a little brief authority,
> Most ignorant of what he's most assured,
> His glassy essence, like an angry ape
> Plays such fantastic tricks before high heaven
> As makes the angels weep; who, with our spleens,
> Would all themselves laugh mortal.   [114–23]

Isabella speaks of the human condition in general, the absurdity of man's posturing before the ultimate judgement which awaits every man, but there is a more immediate personal application. Angelo in his new robes of state exercising authority in the short period before the Duke's return is also 'Dressed in a little brief authority'. It is one of the most trenchant images in the play and one which has been picked up in at least one recent production.

Angelo does not interrupt, and in his increasing involvement allows Isabella a virtual monologue of twenty-five lines in which she again asks that Angelo look for fellow feeling with Claudio:

> Go to your bosom,
> Knock there, and ask your heart what it doth know
> That's like my brother's fault; if it confess
> A natural guiltiness such as is his,
> Let it not sound a thought upon your tongue
> Against my brother's life.   [136–41]

This earnest wish that Angelo admit that he is tainted with original sin forces him to confess the effect Isabella is having on him:

> (*aside*)   She speaks, and 'tis
> Such sense that my sense breeds with it.   [141–2]

For the first time in the play Angelo changes his mind, asking Isabella to return the next day. He guiltily misunderstands Isabella's talk of a bribe and her unworldly reference to the devout prayers of nuns emphasises her spirituality at a moment when we are becoming aware of the sensual effect of her words. In this atmosphere innocent words take on a sexual charge: 'Heaven keep your honour safe', 'God save your honour' [157, 161].

Angelo's inner turmoil immediately breaks out in the first soliloquy of the play, an outcry in which two thirds of the speech are taken up with impassioned questions. Angelo falls into a legalistic frame of thought, trying to assess the degree of culpability between himself and Isabella: 'Is this her fault or mine?'[162]. He concludes that he is the guilty party and indulges in self-debasing images, comparing himself with rotting flesh and his behaviour with that of a sacrilegious despoiler. In the eleven questions of the first part of the soliloquy he is obliged to question the proud image of himself as an impersonal administrator of justice.

After this feverish bout of self-examination the final eight lines of the speech are more reflective as Angelo tries to answer his own questions. He briefly creates a new image for himself, a St Jerome figure tempted by a virtuous woman. But references to the sexual expertise of prostitutes ally Angelo with the sexual underworld of *Measure for Measure* and he is forced to admit that he must give over the complacent detachment with which he has hitherto viewed human frailty.

From Angelo's first words in II iv we realise that he is still in spiritual turmoil. With the praying and the discreet knocking of a servant we surmise we are now in private apartments. We have moved from a public interview to a more intimate exchange of feelings.

Since meeting Isabella Angelo feels unable to sustain his old mode of behaviour, which he now regards as a pose:

> The state, wheron I studied,
> Is like a good thing, being often read,

> Grown seared and tedious; yea, my gravity,
> Wherein, let no man hear me, I take pride,
> Could I, with boot, change for an idle plume
> Which the air beats for vain.   [II iv 7–12]

As the earlier soliloquy recalled the sexual merchants of the play, so here we are reminded of the careless libertines of Vienna such as Lucio, who may actually be wearing the 'idle plume'. This potential transformation of his former self brings Angelo to realise the distinction, pointed out to him earlier by Isabella, between the awesome trappings of power and the fragile nature within:

> O place, O form,
> How often dost thou with thy case, thy habit,
> Wrench awe from fools, and tie the wiser souls
> To thy false seeming!   [12–15]

In this central scene of revelation Angelo is conscious of the dichotomy between the public virtue of the official and the diabolical monster into which he imagines he is being transformed.

At first Angelo is nervous, uncertain how to proceed with Isabella in his new role. He approaches his sexual proposition by several oblique routes, his first method being to trap Isabella into minimising fornication in general. Angelo's speech beginning 'Ha! fie, these filthy vices' has all the sham indignation of the prosecuting lawyer's speech to the jury, a provocative presentation of the argument against unlawful sexual intercourse. Isabella walks into the trap by conceding that fornication may carry strong moral opprobrium in heaven 'but not on earth'. Angelo moves on, exploiting this loop-hole by asking Isabella to consider an apparently abstract question:

> Which had you rather, that the most just law
> Now took your brother's life, or to redeem him
> Give up your body to such sweet uncleanness
> As she that he hath stained?   [52–5]

Angelo's question is logical enough after Isabella's admission that fornication is a venial sin, and she now goes further by confessing that her body's sanctity is of less importance than that of her soul.

The argument seems to be going Angelo's way, but conducted on this abstract level both parties have been led into a blind alley of cross purposes. When Angelo, continuing to talk in generalised terms ('I, now the voice of the recorded law . . .'), brings up the question of a 'charity in sin' which might save Claudio's life, Isabella interprets his remark as applying to the judge's sin in waiving a just sentence. This prompts her into another unworldly outburst promising the grateful prayers of a nun if he will yield to this 'sin' of mercy. Exasperated by what he takes to be Isabella's deliberate refusal to understand the drift of his argument Angelo transfers to the object of his lust a mask of innocence:

> Your sense pursues not mine. Either you are ignorant,
> Or seem so craftily; and that's not good.   [74–5]

He therefore proposes to speak 'more gross', a reference to the directness of his approach and the crudeness of his suggestion.

In fact his second exposition is as oblique as his first, and, having been presented this idea of a sexual offer twice, Isabella breaks out in an ecstatic image of herself as virgin martyr:

>   were I under the terms of death,
>   Th' impression of keen whips I'd wear as rubies,
>   And strip myself to death as to a bed
>   That long I have been sick for, ere I'd yield
>   My body up to shame.   [100–4]

The erotic implications are obvious but theatrically the effect of her passion is to drive her into a ringingly definitive statement of her position:

>   Better it were a brother died at once
>   Than that a sister, by redeeming him,
>   Should die for ever.   [106–8]

It is the most striking example of the wordplay on 'sister', a

total submersion of the blood relationship in Isabella's
membership of a religious order. We can only admit the justice
of Angelo's question:

> Were not you then as cruel as the sentence
> That you have slandered so?   [109–10]

When Angelo points out that earlier Isabella had belittled
Claudio's sin, he makes an effective ploy and Isabella is obliged
to withdraw from her position of utter intransigence. She
engagingly admits that in pleading for her brother she may
have been moved to overstate her case:

> O pardon me, my lord; it oft falls out
> To have what we would have, we speak not what we mean.
> I something do excuse the thing I hate
> For his advantage that I dearly love.   [117–20]

But it is this touching admission of her humanity which allows
Angelo to spring his final trap. At first he appears to release the
highly charged atmosphere with the apparently trite remark,
'We are all frail' [121]. Off her guard Isabella expansively
agrees, admitting that women are notoriously frail. The
admission gives Angelo his opening:

> I do arrest your words. Be that you are,
> That is, a woman; if you be more, you're none.
> If you be one, as you are well expressed
> By all external warrants, show it now,
> By putting on the destined livery.   [134–8]

With this, his closest approach to romantic gallantry, Isabella
begins to suspect that Angelo's arguments hitherto may have
had a personal application and she begs him to return to
abstractions. Angelo counters by directly putting his sexual
bargain but even now Isabella can only accept its crude reality
when Angelo swears by his honour. After numerous
misunderstandings, confusions, and argumentative blind
alleys, both Isabella and Angelo can only find release in violent
language:

> Ha! Little honour to be much believed,
> And most pernicious purpose. Seeming, seeming!
> I will proclaim thee, Angelo, look for't!
> Sign me a present pardon for my brother,
> Or with an outstretched throat I'll tell the world
> What man thou art.   [149–54]

Far from being a passive victim Isabella is stung into rage by her realisation that Angelo has entrapped her in ethical discussion and Angelo in turn is aroused to a counter-threat of the greatest brutality:

> I have begun,
> And now I give my sensual race the rein.
> Fit thy consent to my sharp appetite,
> Lay by all nicety and prolixious blushes,
> That banish what they sue for. Redeem thy brother
> By yielding up thy body to my will,
> Or else he must not only die the death,
> But thy unkindness shall his death draw out
> To lingering sufferance. Answer me tomorrow,
> Or, by the affection that now guides me most,
> I'll prove a tyrant to him. As for you,
> Say what you can, my false o'erweighs your true.   [159–70]

After a scene of oblique arguing Angelo's directness reveals a man who has totally rejected his old pose of gravity and objectivity. This new Angelo, glorying in his role as sexual tyrant, has released the brutal animal energies which the Duke was anxious to restrain through the enforcement of law.

Faced with rampaging lust and frustrated in her anger, Isabella now withdraws into moral absurdity, creating an inhuman image of her brother as a high-minded paragon, of whom we have hitherto seen no sign:

> Though he hath fall'n by prompture of the blood,
> Yet hath he in him such a mind of honour
> That, had he twenty heads to tender down
> On twenty bloody blocks, he'd yield them up,
> Before his sister should her body stoop
> To such abhored pollution.   [178–83]

This Claudio is a suitable companion figure to her virgin martyr. Isabella's notorious couplet

> Then, Isabel, live chaste, and, brother, die.
> More than our brother is our chastity   [184–5]

is the climactic point in this fantastic picture. Its over-neat, epigrammatic quality warns us that Isabella is striving to persuade herself that this brother is not a creature of flesh and blood. As in the convent of St Clare, Isabella is again trying to wrap herself away from the realities of human nature.

6   INTO THE DARKNESS: THE PRISON SCENE, III i

As Isabella leaves the stage, the subject of her soliloquy appears before us, a real human Claudio trying to come to terms with death whilst maintaining a little hope of reprieve:

> The miserable have no other medicine
> But only hope:
> I have hope to live, and am prepared to die.   [III i 2–4]

The Duke's speech in which he prepares Claudio for death is one of the great set pieces in Shakespeare. Though he speaks in his recently assumed role of Friar, the Duke's words are notable for their total lack of Christian reference; most strikingly, there is no mention of the heavenly consolation awaiting the repentant sinner. The speech in fact is an address to life. In its length and stateliness it provides a lower pitch of emotional intensity than either the preceding or ensuing scene, but in terms of plot and the intermingling relations of Isabella, Claudio and Angelo it is irrelevant. We must look to the characterisation of the Duke and its place in his development for its justification. In his earlier scenes we have encountered a kindly but withdrawn and ineffectual ruler, nervously wishing to remain on hand to check on Angelo's behaviour. Now disguised as a friar he can stand back from himself and observe the variety of human nature in his city. His speech to Claudio is in the traditional *contemptus mundi* mode, a rejection of the pleasures of life, but also a powerful poetic account of that theme from a man exploring for himself man's uncertain and fluid nature:

> Thou art not thyself,
> For thou exists on many a thousand grains
> That issue out of dust. Happy thou art not,
> For what thou hast not, still thou striv'st to get,
> And what thou hast, forget'st. Thou art not certain,
> For thy complexion shifts to strange effects,
> After the moon.   [19–24]

This is the base from which the Duke can develop an understanding of human nature, and the justice such a nature demands: human frailty will need eclectic flexible treatment.

Isabella begins her difficult interview with Claudio with the same riddling language that characterised Angelo's first hesitant approaches to her:

> Lord Angelo, having affairs to heaven,
> Intends you for his swift ambassador,
> Where you shall be an everlasting leiger.
> Therefore your best appointment make with speed;
> Tomorrow you set on.   [60–4]

In his sister's presence the stoical pose which Claudio assumed after the Duke's noble words begins to crumble and his first replies to Isabella are half-lines of intense entreaty as he searches for a possible escape route. Isabella is at first less than explicit about the nature of Angelo's proposal, and her circumlocutions put off the moment when she will have to accept that Claudio is not the impossible creature of her imagination. Already as his questions become more insistent the image begins to falter:

> O, I do fear thee, Claudio, and I quake
> Lest thou a feverous life shouldst entertain,
> And six or seven winters more respect
> Than a perpetual honour. Dar'st thou die?   [77–80]

Her words provoke Claudio into adopting his most courageous stance, a pose he takes on in a rush of bravura rhetoric:

> Why give you me this shame?
> Think you I can a resolution fetch
> From flowery tenderness? If I must die,
> I will encounter darkness as a bride,
> And hug it in mine arms.   [84–8]

This is the Claudio Isabella wished to hear, an heroic counterpart to her own saintly chastity:

> There spake my brother. There my father's grave
> Did utter forth a voice. Yes, thou must die.
> Thou art too noble to conserve a life
> In base appliances.   [89–92]

Claudio's tone continues resolute but we hear no more of the bravura note, and his interjections as Isabella explains Angelo's plan are clipped and unexpansive. Isabella again detects some weakening, and, as her illusions prove impossible to preserve and the scene changes direction, we reach in the condemned prisoner's black depression the darkest point of *Measure for Measure*.

Claudio's descent into despair proceeds by way of contemplating the power of sexuality in penetrating the apparently frigid virtue of Angelo:

> Has he affections in him
> That thus can make him bite the law by th'nose,
> When he would force it? Sure it is no sin,
> Or of the deadly seven it is the least. . . .
> If it were damnable, he being so wise,
> Why would he for the momentary trick
> Be perdurably fined?   [111–18]

In questioning for the first time the justice of his sentence and realising that Angelo has now succumbed to the same 'momentary trick' which is taking him to the block, Claudio's fragile resolution shatters:

O Isabel!
ISABELLA. What says my brother?
CLAUDIO.   Death is a fearful thing.
ISABELLA. And shamèd life a hateful.
CLAUDIO. Ay, but to die, and go we know not where,
          To lie in cold obstruction and to rot . . . .   [118–22]

In this famous speech we have the perfervid imagination of a
man within hours of a violent death, contemplating with
horrified fascination his fate in the afterlife. It is another pagan
picture which powerfully counterpoints the Duke's more
confident speech; Claudio's evocation of the horrors after death
leads to an extolment of brute existence at any price:

          The weariest and most loathèd worldly life
          That age, ache, penury, and imprisonment
          Can lay on nature is a paradise
          To what we fear of death.   [132–5]

This natural fear in the face of inevitable death arouses Isabella
to loathing disgust, her illusions about her brother totally
destroyed as her rigid morality refuses to accept him at his most
vulnerable:

                    O you beast!
          O faithless coward! O dishonest wretch!
          Wilt thou be made a man out of my vice?   [139–41]

As her tirade continues Isabella reaches the point of absurdity
when she fervently prays to impugn the chastity of her mother:

          Heaven shield my mother played my father fair,
          For such a warpèd slip of wilderness
          Ne'er issued from his blood.   [144–6]

The father whom earlier in the scene Isabella had heard speak
from the grave in Claudio's defence is now denied paternity of
the same son, and in order to give credence to his feelings
Isabella is obliged to pray that her mother committed adultery.
In the climax of her anger she leaves Claudio to his fate, and her
imagery squarely associates him with the sexual underworld:

> O, fie, fie, fie!
> Thy sin's not accidental, but a trade.
> Mercy to thee would prove itself a bawd,
> 'Tis best that thou diest quickly.   [151–5]

In this impassioned rejection of a brother by a sister *Measure for Measure* reaches its bitter centre point and it is at this moment that (in the words of the Second Folio's stage direction) the 'Duke steps in'. The intricate intrigue and counter-plotting against Angelo begins.

Let us briefly look forward through the rest of the scene (and its continuation in III ii) for what we learn of the Duke's character. At first we see his new penchant for intrigue as he introduces the former history of Angelo and Mariana. He observes the clumsy workings of justice in the front line as Elbow effects Angelo's new policy by arresting Pompey and Overdone. The first scene with Lucio shows us a more human Duke who can, moreover, appreciate, however testily, the problems that confront authority when it ventures outside its immediate sphere. His meeting with Escalus counterpoints the Lucio scene and provides the Duke with a more reliable assessment at a moment when his self-examination is most apparent: the Duke was 'One that, above all other strifes, contended especially to know himself' [III ii 222–3].

In the course of a long scene the Duke has commented as Friar on the fluidity of human nature, he has witnessed the clash of Isabella's inflexible morality with her brother's uncomplicated wish to cling to life; he has seen evidence of Angelo's regime in the arrest of a pimp and a madam, and has been reminded by Lucio of the calumnies which attach themselves to rulers who live secluded lives. More positively, Lucio's teasing has presented us with a sexuality virile Duke, as liable to temptation as Claudio or Lucio, a man competent to handle the counter-attack which will involve lies, and pain to the innocent. Absolute justice, the Duke reflects in his concluding soliloquy, can only be administered by saints:

> He who the sword of heaven will bear
> Should be as holy as severe.   [249–50]

In anybody less than a saint, the judge's frailties will inevitably colour his judgements, and in Angelo's case, where frailty has been denied beneath an iron exterior of virtue, the results may be catastrophic:

> O, what may man within him hide,
> Though angel on the outward side? [259–60]

In this confused and frequently corrupt world, the Duke summarises the plan of action which he has already initiated with Isabella:

> Craft against vice I must apply.
> With Angelo tonight shall lie
> His old betrothèd, but despised:
> So disguise shall by th' disguised
> Pay with falsehood, false exacting,
> And perform an old contracting. [265–70]

The Duke will be obliged to employ a new eclectic strategy to catch Angelo: an intrigue against the intriguer, deception against the deceiver.

7 'CRAFT AGAINST VICE': A CONCLUSION IN WHICH LITTLE IS CONCLUDED

The finale of *Measure for Measure* takes place in the open air near the gates of Vienna with the people of the city in attendance. Whereas many earlier scenes in the play have been set in confined spaces – private chambers, a moated grange, a prison, a nunnery – the action has now been opened out physically at the same time as men's private behaviour is being publically revealed. The previously retiring Duke will conclude his examination of the workings of justice under the scrutiny of the crowd and to the sound of trumpets.

   The scene then proceeds to 'proclaim/Favours that keep within' [v i 15–16] in the complex unravelling of the intrigue, a

process made more complicated by the Duke's wish to entrap
Angelo and hide from Isabella the news that her brother is alive.
Isabella has completely committed herself to the intrigue and
she will lie when it becomes necessary:

> after much debatement
> My sisterly remorse confutes mine honour,
> And I did yield to him.   [v i 99–101]

The Duke, again disguised as Friar, can comment on his former
shortcomings as Duke and the corrupting influence of his
apathy:

> I have seen corruption boil and bubble
> Till it o'errun the stew. Laws for all faults,
> But faults so countenanced that the strong statutes
> Stand like the forfeits in a barber's shop,
> As much in mock as mark.   [316–20]

We are reminded of the Duke's words to Friar Thomas at the
outset, but now his words have lost their intellectual
detachment and are charged with personal observation. The
vigour of this speech continues when Lucio finally 'discovers'
him and the Duke immediately takes charge of the situation
despatching Angelo for marriage to Mariana. But after this
masterful start he reverts to oblique methods when he
continues to maintain to Isabella that Claudio has been
executed. Any credible explanation for this behaviour must be
sought in the Duke's speech which follows the return of Angelo
and his new bride. Angelo is condemned not, in the first
instance, for his attack on Isabella's chastity, which she 'must
pardon/For Mariana's sake', but because Angelo broke his
word and did not release Claudio after sleeping with Isabella:

> as he adjudged your brother,
> Being criminal, in double violation
> Of sacred chastity, and of promise-breach,
> Thereon dependent, for your brother's life,
> The very mercy of the law cries out
> Most audible, even from his proper tongue,
> 'An Angelo for Claudio, death for death!'

Haste still pays haste, and leisure answers leisure,
Like doth quit like, and Measure still for Measure.
Then, Angelo, thy faults thus manifested,
Which, though thou wouldst deny, denies thee vantage,
We do condemn thee to the very block
Where Claudio stooped to death, and with like haste.
Away with him.   [400–13]

For the only time in the play the Duke speaks in the ringing high rhetoric of a Shakespearean ruler, underlined by the striking couplet which contains the play's title. But it is a hollow rhetoric: the Duke knows that Angelo did not go to bed with Isabella and that Claudio was not executed. The neat parallelism of legal sentences on Angelo and his victim falls apart.

As has often been pointed out, the phrase 'measure for measure' is an echo of verses from the Sermon on the Mount: 'Judge not, that ye be not judged. For with what judgment ye judge, ye shall be judged: and with what measure ye mete, it shall be measured to you again' (Matthew 7: 1–2). It is less frequently noted that the Duke's words fly in the face of the spirit and substance of Jesus's sermon and his demand for a less legalistic approach to justice and morality. The Duke's command that Angelo be beheaded on 'the very block/Where Claudio stooped to death' is in line with the unfulfilled law of the Old Testament with its exact equation of crime and punishment: 'He that killeth any man shall surely be put to death. . . . And if a man cause a blemish in his neighbour; as he hath done, so shall it be done to him; Breach for breach, eye for eye, tooth for tooth: as he hath caused a blemish in a man, so shall it be done to him again' (Leviticus 24: 17, 19–20). The Duke's speech is rooted in the legal philosophy within which Angelo has been working, and his words should be seen in part as a challenge to Isabella. Will the New Testament sentiments she proclaimed when pleading for her brother extend to pleading for his judicial murderer?

The Duke has placed the problem in front of her and for thirty lines Isabella keeps silent. At last, after a blunt restatement of the 'measure for measure' legalism ('He dies for Claudio's death' [440]) Isabella goes down on her knees. Her

speech for her brother's murderer and her would-be seducer is
eloquent but reasonable; her belief that 'a due sincerity
governed his deeds/Till he did look on me' [442–4] is a fair
description of Angelo in office and Isabella admits that her
brother was justly condemned. Isabella has justified in action
her Christian beliefs, but even at this climactic moment the
contradictions in this most ambiguous of plays continue. For
the Duke refuses to accept the Christ-like appeals of Isabella
and Mariana and turns to castigating the Provost for
mishandling Claudio's execution. It is only when Claudio is
brought on and the silent reconciliation with Isabella takes place
that the Duke pardons Angelo. And he is pardoned not for the
morality which Isabella now embodies in words and actions but
simply because Claudio is still alive:

> By this Lord Angelo perceives he's safe;
> Methinks I see a quickening in his eye.
> Well, Angelo, your evil quits you well.   [491–3]

Isabella and Mariana have not revealed an alternative view of
justice to the Duke: Angelo is given a pardon for murder simply
because no murder has been committed. He is released in effect
on a writ of *habeas corpus*. Furthermore, by now there is a further
ambiguity in the Duke's behaviour, as he has made the first of
his two proposals of marriage and is anxious to ingratiate
himself with Isabella. His final act of judgement is quite
clear-cut. Although Lucio's original sentence arises out of
pique at his lies, the Duke's 'apt remission' of mercy extends to
his slanderer and Lucio is ordered to marry his whore. If we
gallantly regard Kate Keepdown as a wronged woman, all the
ladies receive justice from the Duke through marriage.

By any strict code of justice the Duke's list of judgements is
inconsistent and inequitable, but it does represent a kind of
natural justice in its allocation of rewards and punishments.
The two humane legal men, Escalus and the Provost, are
promised promotion and Claudio is obliged to marry Juliet.
Angelo does not receive any legal punishment, but he has been
obliged to undergo examination of his sexual conduct, and the
gravity in which he took such pride has now been exposed
before the world. Lucio confesses that his marriage sentence is

worse than the technical penalty of pressing, whipping and hanging: a free-wheeling libertine is condemned to a woman who will make him a subject of ridicule and disdain.

For the Duke's own marital fate the text gives no clear indication. How Isabella responds to his request to forget the nunnery and become the first lady of Vienna is a matter which has to be left to directors, actors and actresses. The only clue we might draw from the text is that the Duke makes his proposal twice, Isabella is given no lines in reply, and on both occasions the Duke hurries on to discuss other matters.

8 THE DUKE VERSUS ANGELO: THE CONSTRUCTION OF 'MEASURE FOR MEASURE'

In few plays of Shakespeare is there such a sudden change of direction as in *Measure for Measure*, and a change moreover which can be pinpointed precisely. At the moment in iii i when the Duke steps out of the shadows he ceases to be an observer and moralist and involves himself in the tangled lives of Angelo, Isabella and Claudio. The effect of the first half of the play has been created by a series of emotional encounters between Angelo and Isabella, the Duke and Claudio, Claudio and Isabella, conducted in verse which is often involved and dense with imagery; the second part is marked by intrigue and black comedy, most of which is written in prose until the finale.

Our point of departure hitherto has been the character of the Duke and his development from ineffective impotence to agile, pragmatic manipulator. There is a clear sense in which the construction reflects this development. After seeming to leave Vienna in haste, the Duke leaves the stage for three long powerful scenes. Our attention is directed to Angelo, the new ducal figure who is cleaning up Vienna. The mood of the Duke's old Vienna is established by the gentlemen of i ii, idle soldiers far from war, vegetating and inwardly rotting with sexual diseases. Into this sickly, lethargic group breaks a second-hand report about the new sex laws, and Angelo's new regime introduces a dynamism into the language and action of the play which is only briefly halted by the intricacies of the Froth–Elbow-Pompey scene. With the intrusion of Isabella into Angelo's life, the pace decelerates as the deputy analyses his behaviour in two reflective soliloquies.

Although the Duke will eventually take up Angelo's forward-thrusting role, his first appearance as Friar is uncertain and tentative. Juliet is humble and dignified in the face of his conventional religiosity. This is still the Duke who dithered over his decision to leave, and his status as an observer of the action continues throughout his famous interview with Claudio, leaving the dynamic of the action with Angelo. Indeed, the Duke's long sermon in III i is the dead-point in the play's construction: a stately stripping-away of illusions to a point from which the plot, now urged on by a newly inspired Duke, again moves forward.

That plot is conduced in prose which Sir Arthur Quiller-Couch characterises as 'euphuistic lingo'. Further, he describes the central scene III i as possessing 'halves [which] cannot be made of a piece by any one possessing even a rudimentary acquaintance with English prose and poetry'. No such disjunction is I think apparent in the theatre, only a change of pace and direction as the Duke unfolds his plot:

> To the love I have in doing good a remedy presents itself. I do make myself believe that you may most uprightteously do a poor wronged lady a merited benefit, redeem your brother from the angry law, do no stain to your own gracious person, and much please the absent Duke, if peradventure he shall ever return to have hearing of this business.   [III i 200–6]

The clauses tumble out from a man newly committed to action, carrying Isabella and the audience along in a new, vitalised path. Angelo, who has hitherto brought a young man's energy to bear on a decadent city, is now removed from the stage; he remains an off-stage presence for the next third of *Measure for Measure*, a depersonalised tyrant or a fumbling lecher. Even in Lucio's monstrous lies we perceive a more potent Duke contrasted in Lucio's fertile imagination with the cold sterility of Angelo.

The only obstacle to the Duke's progress is Barnadine, and

his obstinate pigheadedness is therefore the more memorable and amusing. Some of the pleasure which audiences always derive from Barnadine's short intrusion into the action comes from a realisation that for once not everything is progressing as the Duke would wish. He approaches Barnadine in the same spirit as he had Claudio: 'induced by my charity, and hearing how hastily you are to depart, I am come to advise you, comfort you, and pray with you' [48–50]. But Barnadine's responses are a good deal less vacillating than Claudio's and the Duke is not even allowed the courtesy of a *contemptus mundi* sermon:

> DUKE. . . . I beseech you look forward on the journey you shall go.
> BARNADINE. I swear I will not die today for any man's persuasion.
> DUKE. But hear you.
> BARNADINE. Not a word. If you have anything to say to me, come to my ward, for thence will not I today. (*Exit*) [IV iii 55–61]

The Duke's plans have been bustling forward with so few obstacles that Barnadine's delightfully uncomplicated wish not to have his head chopped off for the convenience of the intrigue gives an audience momentary pleasure in this temporary check to the Duke's plans.

But it is a hitch which, once Barnadine is comfortably back in his straw, draws in the Provost as another member of the counter-plot. With his suggestion that the head of a dead pirate might be opportunely used, we are led to expect a conventional happy ending, with the triumphant return of the Duke and the unmasking and punishment of Angelo.

That triumphant return – a resumption of power temporarily laid aside before punishing evil-doers and rewarding virtue – was, we have seen, one of the plot devices on which Shakespeare drew for the creation of the Duke's character. In terms of the play's construction it shares in importance with what we might call the 'return of the king' folk theme. Vincentio entering Vienna to the sound of trumpets and amongst crowds of citizens may appear like a *deus ex machina*, but he is a god whose mysterious ways we have been allowed to watch and who has depended on others to help him carry out his tasks. Some of the excitement and anticipation of the return may arise from its parallel with the Second Coming, and the

New Testament parables which allude to it: 'After a long time the lord of those servants cometh, and reckoneth with them' (Matthew 26:19).

Shakespeare uses various pieces of stage-craft to call on our anticipated pleasure in a return to ducal power which, we are led to believe, will in turn give Angelo his just deserts. A little scene such as IV v, when the Duke despatches various named servants, builds up our sense of expectation. Our one glimpse of Angelo before the finale shows a dispirited nervous figure who contrasts both with his earlier role of bright-eyed legal eagle and with the rejuvenated Duke.

But after this masterly build-up the finale is not in fact the standard meting-out of rewards and punishments: the Duke's judgements are partial and subjectively arrived at, albeit based on a kind of rough justice. Samuel Johnson speaks for many when he contemplates the uneasy sense of expectations unfulfilled on the final treatment of Angelo: 'Every reader feels some indignation when he finds him spared.' Shakespeare has deliberately led us to expect a different kind of conclusion: in place of the punishments of a satirical Jonsonian comedy we are given one more fitting the ambiguous, messy world of tragi-comedy. By reversing the usual notions of comic justice Shakespeare asks us to concur in a feeling that such clear-cut judgements are not applicable in the world of *Measure for Measure*. There is little doubt that the Angelo of the first half of the play would have dealt with the later transgressor in a fashion which any Johnsonian (or Jonsonian) moralist would have approved. But at the end of his adventures in the underworld of Vienna the Duke is unable to see the relevance of text-book justice for the confused, ambiguous human beings he found there.

9 'NOVELTY IS ONLY IN DEMAND': THE MODERNITY OF 'MEASURE FOR MEASURE'

Of all Shakespeare's plays *Measure for Measure* needs the least special pleading as to its contemporary relevance. Because of its tone, subject matter and language, it is today amongst the more frequently performed and discussed of the plays. Contemporary investigative journalism into politics, sex and corruption, and their not-infrequent interrelations, have done nothing to diminish this transparent contemporaneity. But there are important senses in which regarding *Measure for Measure* as a 'Play for Today' can hinder an appreciation of Shakespeare's complex vision. To dismiss, as some critics suggest, the term 'problem play' as unhelpful does not mean that *Measure for Measure* does not contain problems. An over-simplified view of the play on the stage or in the study after all would be to see the world like an Angelo or an Isabella rather than to share Shakespeare's eschewal of easy solutions and judgements. The world of *Measure for Measure* is one in which a deputising ruler imposes a rigid framework of justice into which human nature is required to fit; when the ruler himself returns at the end of the play, his own judgements reflect a grey world of confusing ambiguities. The moral and legal certainties of Angelo and Isabella have shipwrecked on the rocks of human fallibility, and the Duke is left to pick out pragmatic solutions as best he can.

Facing the fact that *Measure for Measure* is a difficult play is a reasonable first step for the student and director. With the confidence of contemporary wisdom one should avoid the temptation to cut through at least two potential Gordian knots which are best left tangled.

The first 'knot' is the old problem of Isabella's chastity. This has traditionally been regarded as one of the problems of *Measure for Measure* which demands an answer. Is Isabella right to refuse to go to bed with Angelo in order to save her brother, and, if she is wrong, what sort of heroine does this make her? That she *is* wrong would seem to be received opinion today. Isabella's attachment to the virtues of the convent is fallible and leads her into moral absurdity and cruelty, but those virtues in themselves are not derisible. Her standards collapse when she is compelled to employ them in a confrontation in which Angelo uses all his guile to allow her no possible escape route. The issue of Isabella's chastity might be more appropriately considered alongside Angelo's guilt in placing her in the dilemma in the first place. To ask why Isabella should be obliged to submit herself to a man for whom she feels only contempt is a response which has risen out of the feminist perspective of the last twenty years. Certainly a narrow image of Isabella as a self-righteous prig will belittle Shakespeare's portrait of a young, immature woman desperately trying to wrap herself within the values of the nunnery.

A more general area of unease arises out of the moral relativity of the law-givers and law-breakers. That Shakespeare portrays his two principle moral absolutists as fallible is self-evident, but we should remember the impact made by Escalus and the Provost, men who attempt to administer humane justice on the law-makers' side of the judicial divide. Isabella's Christian rhetoric is triumphantly made real when she kneels for the man who she believes has killed her brother. Even Angelo before his catastrophic meeting with Isabella shows a refreshing desire to tone up the moral flaccidity of Vienna. Conversely, it is not easy to see how the sex merchants of the city possess any life-enhancing virtues which their betters lack, the 'joyous vitality of the clowns' which Herbert S. Weil sees in this group. Pompey, Overdone and Lucio are certainly amusing in their wish to be allowed to get on with their lives without the nuisance of the law-makers' interference, and Lucio is a memorable spokesman for the absurdity of the laws against sexuality. But in their language and attitudes we never forget that the commodity in which these people deal is lust, not love, and the language of pimps, madams and their customers centres around blasphemy, sloth and diseased rottenness. As happens frequently in *Measure for Measure*, we are given no obvious point of moral reference; the sexual underworld of Vienna is clearly in need of some sort of reform, but the unbending absolutism of Angelo will only work when it is administered by saints.

PART TWO: PERFORMANCE

10   INTRODUCTION: THE FOUR MAIN PRODUCTIONS

The four main productions discussed below are as follows.

1. The 1970 Royal Shakespeare Company production at Stratford-upon-Avon directed by John Barton and designed by Timothy O'Brien. Sebastian Shaw was the Duke, Estelle Kohler Isabella, Ian Richardson Angelo, Terrence Hardiman Lucio, Patrick Barr Escalus, Ted Valentine Abhorson.

2. The production adapted and directed by Charles Marowitz at the Open Space Theatre, London in 1975. The designer was Robin Don. Richard Mayes was the Duke, Ciaran Madden Isabella, Nikolas Simmonds Angelo, David Schofield Lucio, Glyn James Escalus, Geoffrey Staines the Bishop, and Brian Gwaspari Claudio.

3. The Royal Shakespeare Company production directed by Barry Kyle and first staged at Stratford in 1978. The designer was Christopher Morley. The Duke was played by Michael Pennington, Angelo by Jonathan Pryce, Isabella by Paola Dionisotti, Pompey by Richard Griffiths, Lucio by John Nettles, Escalus by Raymond Westwell, Elbow by Geoffrey Freshwater, and Barnadine by Conrad Asquith.

4. The production for the BBC Television Shakespeare directed by Desmond Davis and broadcast on 18 February 1979. The production was designed by Stuart Walker. Kenneth Colley played the Duke, Kate Nelligan Isabella, Tim Piggott-Smith Angelo, John McEnery Lucio, Frank Middlemass Pompey.

A word on the choice of productions. These were selected to provide a representative selection of good productions during an important period of *Measure for Measure*'s stage history. However, the play has been well staged on several occasions since the Second World War and references will occasionally be made to other productions when they cast light on a particular view of the play. I do not wish to suggest that they constitute a 'second division'; they include distinguished work by Peter Brook (Shakespeare Memorial Theatre, 1950), John Retallack for the Actors' Touring Company production of 1980, and Michael Rudman for the Caribbean production at the National Theatre in 1981.

11   'MEASURE FOR MEASURE' BEFORE 1970

Before considering the main productions we need to look briefly at the play's stage history before 1970 to account for its burst of popularity in the last fifteen years.

Measure for Measure has had a scrappy stage history. Following its only recorded performance in Shakespeare's lifetime in 1604, the play was not staged in anything like its original form for over a century. At the Restoration it suffered the usual risible attempts at 'improvement', Sir William D'Avenant combining elements from the play with Beatrice and Benedict story from *Much Ado about Nothing* and calling the new compilation *The Law against Lovers*. In 1700 Charles Gildon brought out an adaptation even more ludicrous than D'Avenant's with musical interludes introduced as entertainments laid on by the enterprising Escalus for Angelo's birthday.

Both versions introduce an aspect of *Measure for Measure* which dogged it until well into the twentieth century. D'Avenant and Gildon cut out all low-life characters and, perhaps surprisingly in view of the reputation of the Restoration stage, made the remaining characters more respectable. D'Avenant achieved this remarkable result by having Angelo, perturbed by the low moral standards of women, merely test Isabella. At the conclusion of the play he marries her:

> I'll now at once cast off my whole disguise. . . .
> Since you fully have endur'd the best
> Of all your sex, submissively I woo
> To be your lover, and your Husband too.

Charles Gildon goes further. Before the action of the play begins, Angelo has secretly married Mariana, and to clear up any remaining unpleasantness Claudio has made an honest woman of Juliet. Both adaptors sensed that in *Measure for Measure* there was a disturbing element which a contemporary audience would not accept. In detecting this unsettling aspect of the play in treating sexuality and the precarious nature of law and authority, D'Avenant and Gildon were laying down the foundations for the charges of indecency which critics (and theatre producers) felt bound to consider for the next three centuries.

On the Georgian stage the sexual underworld only put in an appearance when it was necessary for the working of the main plot. In the acting version of 1777 the second scene opens with the entrance of the disgraced Claudio: the dirty talk of the gentlemen, Lucio, Pompey and Overdone is totally removed. This area of the play has always been subject to cutting and rewriting. In 1803 John Philip Kemble restored some of the racier elements when he played the Duke to his sister Sarah Siddons's Isabella, but there was little of the sub-plot to be seen. Kemble and Siddons were acting at a time when Coleridge was categorising *Measure for Measure* as 'a hateful work ... the single exception to the delightfulness of Shakespeare's plays', and Coleridge's remarks seem to reflect the view of the nineteenth-century audience and the producers who catered for them. Although *Measure for Measure* never, as Bernard Shaw implies, disappeared from the repertoire altogether, its occasional performances tended to be the work of dedicated Shakespeareans. In 1908 William Poel produced the play under Elizabethan stage conditions, a production which bewildered some members of the audience and overwhelmed others. Poel's search for authenticity did not extend to the text: 'bawd' was hardly spoken during the whole performance and the climactic line 'By yielding up thy body to my will' [II iv 164] became the unmetrical 'By yielding up thy self to my will'. Even so some local Stratfordians protested that the play was unfit for representation.

An examination of the repertoire of the Old Vic and Stratford, theatres committed to Shakespeare, reveals that between 1879 and 1914 *Measure for Measure* was performed only three times at Stratford (including the Poel production); between the wars it was only seen twice more. At the Old Vic it appeared only three times. One of these, however, was a distinguished production in 1933 with Charles Laughton and Flora Robson. Even so, the small audiences were commented upon.

If one is to appreciate the play's popularity today it is important to grasp how widespread was the general disgust before the last war. Charles Odell produced his *Shakespeare from Betterton to Irving* in 1921. It is a delightfully idiosyncratic but scholarly book, but on *Measure for Measure* Odell cannot restrain his moral indignation. The main plot is 'revolting', the sub-plot 'exceedingly offensive'. He defends earlier adaptations which cut out the sexual underworld because they have no business on the stage anyway. The Georgian acting version pleases Odell because it was 'fumigated of these people'; 'its being disinfected of the gross underworld folk makes it unusually pleasing'.

Today such attitudes seem quaint and amusing. With increased sexual explicitness in the last quarter of a century, the alleged indecency of *Measure for Measure* is no longer an issue. But it would be naïve to deny that some of its increased popularity is a reaction to this earlier disapproval. It is also worth considering how far our insouciance to stage sexuality has blunted our response to the danger and fear to which D'Avenant, Coleridge and Odell responded.

The first major production after the war was by Peter Brook at Stratford in 1950. It was a seminal treatment of the play which, with Harry Andrews's Duke, Barbara Jefford's Isabella, and John Gielgud's Angelo, established the play as a serious addition to the Shakespeare repertoire. It is significant in view of the play's later history that Brook presented the Duke as a human figure, wise and benevolent, not even Lucio's slanders provoking him to a display of pique. Brook let the three principals play out their passions against a brilliantly represented Viennese underworld, creating, in the procession of prisoners in IV iii, a *coup de théâtre* of which directors have felt necessary to take account ever since.

Brooke's Duke may have been a creature of flesh and blood, but under the influence of academic opinion he became increasingly regarded as embodying a kind of divinity. Even when the crueller aspects of his behaviour could not be ignored, as in John Blatchley's 1962 Stratford production, Tom Fleming's Duke was regarded as a capricious deity presiding over a universe where happiness and pain were incomprehensibly mixed. At the Old Vic in 1963 James Maxwell's Duke walked on stage to be greeted by his courtiers prostrate on the floor, and at the Bristol Old Vic in 1966 Tyrone Guthrie produced what can be seen as the climax to this Duke-as-God-the-Father school of production. Guthrie explained that for him the Duke was 'a figure of Almighty God; a stern and crafty father to Angelo, a stern but kind father to Claudio, an elder brother to the Provost . . . and to Isabella, first a loving father and, eventually the Heavenly Bridegroom to whom at the beginning of the play she was betrothed' (programme note to the production). Despite this portentous build-up, he was also 'a jovially eccentric figure, whirling his crucifix like a propeller' (review in *The Times*, 4 March 1966) and getting caught up in his newly acquired Friar's robes. By the time the earliest of our main productions was staged, in 1970, *Measure for Measure* was carrying this sort of allegorical allusiveness, to which directors were expected to respond. Broadly speaking, *Measure for Measure* in the 1970s underwent a process of demythologising in order to take on a depth of psychological insight and new political and social perspectives.

12 THE MAIN PRODUCTIONS: CONTEXT AND INTERPRETATION

Faced with this stage history, Henry Fenwick in his *Radio Times* introduction to the television production could characterise it as a play which 'has been particularly subject to directorial whim' ('Arguments of State', 10–16 February 1979). Certainly, when confronted by its complexity, many directors have felt compelled to impose a distinct directorial control on its slippery nature. With our four productions we could suggest a spectrum ranging from Davis and the BBC production, where the play was by and large left to make points for itself, through the two RSC versions, to the Marowitz adaptation for the Open Space

Theatre. Superficially a wish to let the play speak for itself seems an attractive idea and, as I pointed out in the Introduction, a dogmatic approach to this most anti-dogmatic of plays can hardly be an appropriate response. The play has to retain its difficulties. But the opposite extreme also presents problems: with no real directorial viewpoint, the play loses any claim to serious attention and an audience is left with what can seem a tiresome mixture of inexplicable behaviour and intrigue. The most effective kind of control would seem to be one which, as Michael Billington observed, 'works through the text rather than imposes an arbitrary concept on it' (*Guardian*, 28 June 1978). The most successful recent productions have taken this approach whilst working out from a crucial, central image of the play.

The BBC TV production (1979)

Some of these problems were highlighted by Desmond Davis's 1979 production for the BBC Television Shakespeare series. *Measure for Measure* was one of the earliest productions in the plan to televise all thirty-seven plays, and Cedric Messina, the producer, was anxious to establish the productions as authoritative and entertaining. 'For students, these productions will offer a wonderful opportunity to study the plays performed by some of the greatest classical actors of our times' (Cedric Messina, Preface to the BBC edition). To give each production authority, they were prefaced by a William Walton fanfare, shots of 'historic England', and the prominent display of the name of a distinguished 'literary adviser', the whole series being presented under the imposing general title, 'The BBC Television Shakespeare'. (Several of these features were dropped later in the series).

The *Measure for Measure* was an intelligent, sensitive account of a play which the director rightly regarded as 'difficult', and which would be unfamiliar to a viewing rather than a theatre-going audience. An understandable wish to get the play across to people approaching it for the first time set its tone, especially in the design elements. The text was hardly touched, costumes and setting were traditional, characterisation was straightforward, and the production was well received. An American critic hailed it as 'the most brilliant success of the series so far . . . the only production . . . that one wants to compare to memorable performances in the theatre' (Maurice Charney, *Shakespeare Quarterly*, 1980). With hindsight one can see that many of the weaknesses which arose from the philosophy of the series – a reverential approach, diverse acting-styles, old-fashioned designs – were avoided. Stuart Walker, the designer, brought to the production a coherency such as marked several later plays in the series, and much of the acting produced scenes of great emotional intensity. But finally it was these impressive moments and tasteful designs with which one was left; they were not enough to compensate for the lack of a central interpretation. The often-quoted disjunction between the parts of the play became apparent, and, after the strength of the confrontation scenes in the first half, eschewing interpretation became a distinct handicap when intrigue and plot take over in the second. Kate Nelligan, the production's Isabella, may well be right when she described earlier productions as ones which 'directors like to get their hands on . . . and do things to', but the trouble with Desmond Davis's *laissez-faire* approach was that one was left with a feeling of mystification. Why did those people behave in such peculiar ways? With no emotional or psychological basis for their behaviour, the play loses its way in a maze of tedious intrigue.

The 1970 RSC production

In both the Kyle and Barton productions the directors let the play get on with its work whilst maintaining a clear view of what it was about. Barton's 1970 production was crafted with a scrupulous attention to detail which meant that nothing happened on the stage, nothing was seen on the stage, which did not contribute to the director's general view of the play.

Since the mid 1960s Barton had concentrated on Shakespearean comedies and had shown an interest in bringing out the darker, more realistic elements in what many people had come to regard as untroubled, high-spirited comedy. The most immediate influence on the 1970 *Measure for Measure* was

Barton's *Twelfth Night* from the previous season. Barton himself makes the connection when he speaks of both plays being ones in which there is 'that sense of reality breaking in on convention . . . where a wry sense of what life's really like and what people are really like is at odds with what the story-line dictates' (interview with Gareth Lloyd Evans in *Aspects of Shakespeare's 'Problem Plays'*). This tension between the conventional form of Shakespeare's play – its movement to what appears to be a resolution – and the realism allegedly breaking out of that convention reaches its climax in Marowitz's treatment of the text five years later. For Barton the moment when 'reality' breaks through had often been in its final stages: the cold air which the messenger Mercade brings in the last scene of his *Love's Labour's Lost* (1965); the callous treatment of Malvolio and the marriage of Sir Toby and Maria in *Twelfth Night*. The most memorable moment in this *Measure for Measure* too, certainly its most commented upon piece of directorial intervention, was Isabella's reaction to the Duke's proposal at the conclusion of the production.

With this concern for realism within the conventional comic form, it is not surprising that Barton broke with the fashion for allegorical productions of the play and made his *Measure for Measure* defiantly anti-symbolic. The Duke of Sebastian Shaw was as far removed as possible from the quasi-deities of the previous decade. Indeed, the root of the problems of *Measure for Measure* seemed to lie in the weakness of Vienna's Duke. Like Henry VI in Barton's *Wars of the Roses*, a power vacuum at the centre caused by an irresolute ruler creates social chaos. By his attachment to the 'life removed' the Duke has isolated himself from his people and their problems. This Duke was just the sort of incompetent judge of character who would choose an Angelo to sort out his city's problems and then hover around to find out if he had made the right decision.

Charles Marowitz (1975)

With Charles Marowitz we are at the furthest point from any non-interventionist view of the play. *Measure for Measure* was the fourth of Marowitz's adaptations, variations or versions of

Shakespearean texts. Usually *Hamlet* (1965), *A Macbeth* (1969) and *The Shrew* (1973) are grouped with this *Measure for Measure*, but they do not in fact share a common purpose. It is more useful to link Marowitz's *Measure for Measure* with other Shakespearean variations of the last twenty years, plays such as Tom Stoppard's *Rosencrantz and Guildenstern are Dead*, Edward Bond's *Lear* and Arnold Wesker's *The Merchant*. These plays give us reworkings of Shakespearean texts 'for our times'; they are not, like the Marowitz versions of *Hamlet* or *Macbeth*, interpretations of the play, but rather attempts to point the plot material in a different direction. The implication is that Shakespeare's vision is inadequate *in his form* for our age. The Marowitz *Measure for Measure* is closer to such a play as Edward Bond's *Lear* of five years earlier with its wish to make Shakespeare's picture of evil more terrible by removing the counter-movements towards love or redemption.

With his version, Marowitz is making a clear, unambiguous statement, and to leave a performance of the play with unresolved feelings would be considered a failure on his part. His adaptation is a plea for justice against law, an exposition of the theme that 'the law is a deadly mechanism by which favour and prejudice are allowed to trample innocence', its path smoothed by 'theatrical assumptions of pomp' (Marowitz in the Introduction to *The Marowitz Shakespeare*). As we shall see, the text is radically reshaped to create rage at the bland corruption and self-satisfaction of the Duke, Escalus and Angelo. Of all the productions, Marowitz's is the least ambiguous in its intentions. That one does not dismiss it out of hand as a shameless over-manipulation of his material can be ascribed to the intellectual agility with which Marowitz puts together his intellectual jigsaw, and because we know that this is *his Measure for Measure* and not Shakespeare's. If, Marowitz wrote in the *Guardian* (28 May 1975), 'our bevy of Shakespearean scholars disagree with his adaptation and hotly contest that it "is not what *Measure for Measure*" is about, he can only reply that "it is as far as I'm concerned" '. It is perhaps Marowitz's sheer gall in quarrying out such a single-minded view of the play that carries us along with him and temporarily puts aside any wish to see a more balanced approach to the play.

The Marowitz version with its savage attack on legalism and its destruction of the individual is the clearest example of one popular view of *Measure for Measure* in the early 1970s. Against a background of Watergate and the moral backlash against the 'permissive' 1960s, *Measure for Measure* was frequently performed as a black satire against establishment corruption and moral hypocrisy. One does not have to look far in programme notes to find obligatory references to and photographs of liberal hate figures of the period. Howard Brenton's version for the Northcott Theatre, Exeter, in 1972 included such contemporary types as a psychiatrist and a corrupt constable, and contrasted Angelo and the Duke as advocates of different brands of Toryism. The viewpoint of these productions and versions is very dark and, though Marowitz speaks of Isabella's fragile humanity being 'still potent enough to destroy the fabric of man-made law', only in her cold rejection of Angelo's final suggestion is there any positive outlet from the grim, closed world he portrays.

The 1978 RSC production

Barry Kyle's 1978 production is a partial turning-away from the satirical visions embodied in productions from earlier in the decade. Some of the force of this version derives from the RSC production of the play which preceded Kyle's. In 1974 Keith Hack's production was greatly influenced by Edward Bond's views on Shakespeare. It was very harshly treated by the critics, and the production certainly seemed intent on ignoring anything which took away from the all-pervasive nastiness of its viewpoint. Something of its flavour can be re-created from the note from Bond to the director quoted in the programme: 'Angelo is a lying, self-deceiving fraud, the Duke a vain face-saving hypocrite and the saintly Isabella a vicious sex hysteric. That is a total arraignment of conventional authority and the morality used to explain and excuse it.' Barry Kyle five years later took over much of the general coarseness of Hack's Vienna, but, in contrast to the cocksure confidence of the Hack–Bond view of its characters, shaped out much of the complex action and patterns of the play. The nastiness of

Viennese life was a starting-point rather than an end in itself. The gentle, inquiring Duke of 1979 seemed a direct reaction to the role as portrayed in 1974, when the Duke was characterised by Bond as 'another Angelo, a public fraud', accepting Lucio as an honest assessor of his moral qualities. Kyle's Duke was not a moral hypocrite, nor was his Angelo a sadistic pharisee. By the end of the play a way forward had been indicated in the Duke's new sense of security, in Isabella's pleasure in her femininity, and in their warm harmonious relationship with each other. Barton and Kyle present contrasting pictures of the play. For Barton it is a closed world of characters locked into their flawed, rigid personalities; for Kyle, the central characters have learnt a little, and at Mariana's grange we glimpse a more fertile world away from the Viennese streets.

13   What the Characters Said: The Texts of Barton, Davis and Kyle

Because of its relative unpopularity before this century, *Measure for Measure* has not been regarded as fruitful material for the adapter. An imaginative Actors' Touring Company production in 1980 directed by John Retallack introduced some topical gagging on the 'law and order' theme and, as noted in the last section, in 1972 Howard Brenton wrote a highly politicised version of the play. But in general the major changes have been made through cutting and the occasional rearrangement of speeches and scenes. Three of the most common areas for this sort of attention are the opening of i ii, the long central prison scenes, and the explanations of the finale. Peter Brook made cuts in all three areas, in order, it was felt, to remove anything which would take away from the authority of his Duke.

Barton's text

The technique employed in both RSC productions was that known as 'thinning' – removing lines and words within speeches to make a more direct and comprehensible text. Thus Barton and Kyle dropped lines – not always the same ones – from long speeches such as Claudio's attempted explanation of Angelo's new policy [I ii155–70] and the Duke's 'measure for measure' speech in the finale [v 397–413]. But the method was most clearly employed in the Duke–Friar's prose expositions to Isabella in the prison scenes. Here is a passage from the Penguin edition:

> Therefore fasten your ear on my advisings. To the love I have in doing good a remedy presents itself. I do make myself believe that you may most uprighteously do a poor wronged lady a merited benefit, redeem your brother from the angry law, do no stain to your own gracious person, and much please the absent Duke, if peradventure he shall ever return to have hearing of this business.   [III i 199–206]

In Barton's text this became:

> Therefore fasten your ear on my advisings. A remedy presents itself. You may redeem your brother, do no stain to your gracious person, and much please the absent Duke.

The prose is leaner, if a little austere, and we might wonder if Sebastian Shaw's Duke would not have been more likely to use the baroque circumlocutions of the original text.

By Kyle's standard, Barton was a vigorous cutter and he can perhaps be faulted for depriving Angelo of half his statement of policy in the speech beginning 'The law hath not been dead, though it hath slept' [II ii 90–9]. The impact of the Duke's 'Be absolute for death' speech was certainly diminished by losing

> Thou art not noble,
> For all th'accommodations that thou bear'st
> Are nursed by baseness   [III i 13–15]

and

> Thou art not thyself,
> For thou exists on many a thousand grains
> That issue out of dust.   [19–21]

By contrast, Kyle cut only the opaque phrase about 'palsied eld' [34–5].

Another technique which Barton employs is his distribution of small sections of lines and speeches to other characters. Sometimes this makes plausible the presence of a totally or relatively silent character in a scene, such as Juliet in I ii. Barton gives her a line and a half of Claudio's–

> on whom it will, it will;
> On whom it will not, so: yet still 'tis just   [I ii 121–2]

– preparing for her dignified submission to the Duke–Friar later.

More importantly, this occasional redistribution created the impression of a wider circle of people involving themselves in the action. The most interesting of Barton's 'new' characters is the unnamed Justice at Pompey's examination, to whom Shakespeare gives only a few non-committal comments. He is brought into the action earlier in the scene by clearing his throat to cast doubt on one of Angelo's legal pronouncements. He also takes over some of Angelo's questions to Pompey. The impression that Angelo is out of step with the rest of the Viennese establishment and that he is not interested in bread-and-butter legal work is intensified. Similar textual reallocation builds up the Provost early in the action as a reluctant administrator of a bad law. To Lucio's question, 'With child, perhaps?' the Provost replies with Claudio's words, 'Unhappily, even so' [I ii 155]. By these tiny adjustments Barton prepared us for the moment – a touching one in his production – when the Provost joins the counter-attack.

The BBC text

Despite the fact that it was aimed at a popular, 'first time Shakespeare' audience, the BBC's production was played with much the fullest text of all the productions. IV iv disappears altogether, a few of Lucio's teasing questions to Pompey in III ii are thinned out, as is Pompey's verbiage in court. But the great pace at which a television version can be taken enabled Davis and his script-editor to play both Angelo–Isabella interviews, the Duke's scene with Claudio, the description of Angelo's murky past, and the whole of the finale, without a single cut. The handful of alterations was caused by the transference from the stage to the small screen, lines being dropped whose business could be done by the cameraman. In the first scene, for example, the Duke announces Angelo's approach with the words 'Look where he comes' [24], highlighting for a theatre audience the arrival of a major new character. On television the gesticulatory line could go and a long tracking shot at the moment of Angelo's entrance substituted.

Sometimes topping and tailing a scene and television's ability to cut cleanly between locations underlined significant juxtapositions. We were taken immediately from Escalus's doubts about the wisdom of Claudio's execution to the Provost arguing a similar case with Angelo (end of II ii to beginning of II iii). The common-sense opposition of two of Vienna's good-natured officers was again emphasised. Barton had done something similar when he reversed the order of I iii and iv. Isabella entered immediately after Lucio and her brother's discussion about her, and the Duke's

> Hence shall we see,
> If power change purpose, what our seemers be   [I iii 53–4]

was delivered as Angelo made his first appearance invested with ducal power.

The texts of the prison scene

The most fundamental changes in all three productions were made in the prison scenes. The BBC left them virtually as printed in the First Folio, but III ii and IV ii were divided up into small scenes played in different locations: outside the prison, in various cells, offices, and corridors within its walls. All three directors increased the impact of the arrest of Mistress Overdone and her whores, the BBC by creating a new brothel scene with some Jacobean-style invective for the furious girls.

John Barton tightened up this area of the play by cutting and shifting speeches, usually in the interests of the Duke's character. His couplet

> That we were all, as some would seem to be,
> Free from our faults, as faults from seeming free   [III ii 36]

was moved forward to follow Isabella's exit at the end of III i, thus becoming a gracious compliment on Isabella's sincerity as much as a criticism of Angelo. Fervently delivered by Sebastian Shaw it was also an indication of the Duke's increasing interest in Isabella as a woman. Barton's second rearrangement clarified one of the curious features of the prison scenes, the Duke's lack of comment when he hears that Angelo has ordered Claudio's execution: a powerful moment in Barton's production in part produced by placing the Duke's speech beginning

> Not so, not so; his life is paralleled
> Even with the stroke and line of his great justice
>   [IV ii 76–82]

immediately before the servant's entrance with the confirmation of Claudio's execution. The speech was a last flickering note of hope that Angelo would keep his word, and the Duke's dismay when the contents of the letter are revealed was intensified.

But the greatest textual alterations here were made by Barry Kyle. The instigation of the counter-plot in the dialogue between Isabella and the disguised Duke was switched to the end of the prison sequence. After interrupting the argument between brother and sister, the Duke, in Kyle's version, indicates that he would like to speak to Isabella, entreating her 'to return again upon the stroke of three'. Isabella goes away and the rest of the episodes take place in their Shakespearean order: the imprisonment of Pompey, Lucio's encounter with the Friar, the round-up of Overdone and her girls, the conversation with Escalus. As Escalus leaves, the clock strikes three, Isabella re-enters and the Duke explains his plan.

This arrangement was theatrically effective in that the prose explanations did not lose impact by following the violent scene with Claudio. Isabella was not required to switch drastically from the impassioned berater of her brother to the Duke's impassive auditor. But the change was most important for its effect on the Duke's development. In Kyle's production his ideas for entrapping Angelo do not come out of the blue; they are formulated as the long procession of newly arrived sex offenders are logged into the prison before the Duke's gaze. His final remark to Escalus, 'If his own life answer the straitness of his proceeding, it shall become his well; wherein if he chance to fail, he hath sentenced himself' [III ii 244–56] becomes more portentous after this vivid presentation of 'the straitness of his proceeding.'

14   WHAT THE CHARACTERS SAID: THE CHARLES MAROWITZ VERSION

With the Marowitz version of *Measure for Measure* it is not a question of cutting the text, changing locales or rearranging scenes. The play contains the familiar Marowitz elements of collage Shakespeare, a text created out of lines, dialogues and scenes from the original text, freely distributed amongst other characters or perversely delivered by the original character to make ironical or interpretative comments on Shakespeare's play. But this sort of metamorphosis does not make up all the text. At first we appear to be watching a condensed studio production with little bits of clever director's business. Escalus was clearly expecting to take over power himself and his subsequent relations with Angelo are strained. A new character, the Bishop, is introduced, another establishment figure preserving the traditional morality which underpins the corrupt legal system. The Bishop is given some of Friar Thomas's lines and some of the Duke's when disguised as a Friar. He delivers the 'Be absolute for death' speech, administering the last rites to Claudio whilst his sister is in bed with Angelo. Up to this crucial plot change Marowitz tried to persuade his audience that they were watching an imaginative fringe production. But this is not a radical

1. John Barton production, 1970. Isabella denounces Angelo before the Duke. *Left to right:* Isabella (Estelle Kohler), Angelo (Ian Richardson) and the Duke (Sebastian Shaw). Photograph © Reg Wilson.

2. Charles Marowitz production, 1975, Claudio leads Isabella to Angelo's bed. *Left to right:* Angelo (Nikolas Simmonds), Claudio (Brian Gwaspari) and Isabella (Ciaran Madden). Photograph © Donald Cooper.

3. Charles Marowitz production, 1975. Isabella (Ciaran Madden) discovers the severed head of her brother after her night with Angelo. Photograph © Donald Cooper.

4. Barry Kyle production, 1978. Isabella (Paola Dionisotti) explains the assignation with Angelo to the Duke (Michael Pennington). Photograph © Joe Cocks Studio.

5. Barry Kyle production, 1978. Angelo (Jonathan Pryce) in his robes of authority confronts Lucio (John Nettles). Photograph © Joe Cocks Studio.

interpretation of Shakespeare's *Measure for Measure* but a critique of the play and its view of society. To achieve this end, the disguised Duke and Mariana are cut, leaving Isabella an isolated victim of a cruel society; Isabella gives herself to Angelo; the deputy has Claudio beheaded. To concentrate attention on the central moral issues of the play, the low-life sub-plot is dropped.

The collage section of the adaptation opens with a taped sequence of lines to which Isabella listens before her sexual encounter with Angelo. In what Marowitz describes as 'a kind of surreal dream sequence' we are given what amounts to a highly abbreviated summary of the happy ending towards which Shakespeare's play in Marowitz's view seems to be heading:

> DUKE (*to the* PROVOST). Look you, sir, here is the hand and seal of the
> Duke. You know the character, I doubt not, and the signet is not
> strange to you.
> PROVOST (*suddenly respectful*). Pardon me, my noble Lord.
> (CLAUDIO *appears and is unmasked by the* PROVOST. *He goes to the* DUKE
> *and kneels*).
> DUKE. Thou'rt condemned.
> But for those earthly faults, I quit them all.
> And pray thee take this mercy to provide
> For better times to come.
> (ISABELLA, *full of gratitude, bows down before the* DUKE.)
> ISABELLA. My noble lord!
> DUKE (*to* ISABELLA). Put yourself not into amazement how these
> things should be. All difficulties are but easy when they are
> known.

Not surprisingly this high-speed caricature is immediately cut away. Angelo is standing back to back with the Duke, Tweedledum and Tweedledee figures whose common corruption becomes increasingly apparent. When the Duke changes places with Angelo, part of the second interview in II iv is rerun, but the ambiguities of Isabella's responses to Angelo, presented by Shakespeare with delicate use of metaphor and innuendo, are developed out in ironic delivery of the dialogue:

> ISABELLA. My brother did love Juliet,
> And you tell me he shall die for't.
> ANGELO. He shall not Isabel, if you give me love.

These lines are to be spoken 'playfully', 'fondly', and at the climax of the scene Angelo and Isabella 'kiss fondly'. To point up Isabella's confused feelings for Angelo, the dialogue in which the Duke–Friar confronts Juliet with her sin [II iii] is transferred to the Bishop and Isabella:

BISHOP. Love you the man that wronged you?
ISABELLA (*pause*). Yes, as I love the woman that wronged him.
BISHOP. So then it seems your most offenceful act
　　Was mutually committed?
ISABELLA. Mutually.

In the encounters between Isabella and Angelo and the Bishop and Isabella, Marowitz has opened up areas of their subconscious life. Another exposure occurs when the incestuous undertones of the interview between brother and sister are laid bare. Their exchanges are now delivered 'archly', 'close', 'smiling seductively'. As Isabella breaks from a lecherous embrace with Claudio, a tape made up of urgent lines and phrases from these rerun scenes takes Isabella up to the moment when she gives herself to Angelo.

At this point Marowitz introduces a new speech for Isabella, his only interpolation of lines not in Shakespeare's play:

Dissolve my life, let not my sense unsettle
Lest I should drown, or stab, or hang myself.
O state of Nature, fail together in me
. Since the best props are warpt. So which way now?
The best way is the next way to a grave.
Each errant step beside is torment. Lo,
The moon is down, the crickets chirp, the screech-owl
Calls in the dawn. All offices are done
Save what I fail in.
An end, and that is all.

The lines are from *The Two Noble Kinsmen*, a work generally regarded as written by Shakespeare in collaboration with John Fletcher. The play is a courtly story of implacable rivalry in love, but Marowitz's speech is taken from the play's sub-plot, in which the Gaoler's Daughter falls in love with Palamon but goes mad when he does not return her affection. For anyone with knowledge of the play, the use of these lines from a character whose love is unashamedly sexual and their transference to the erotically confused Isabella carries an ironical charge. But Marowitz's stated reason for introducing the speech was that Isabella should not be 'deprived of her motivation' for going to bed with Angelo (*Plays and Players*, June 1975). It is questionable whether we learn anything further from the speech than we have heard in the reworked scenes with Angelo, Claudio and the Bishop, and the Gaoler's Daughter's wish to die rather than lose her reason sits uneasily with the confused wishes of Isabella to save her brother.

The final section of this *Measure for Measure* emerges from the collage sequence into a realistic reworking of Shakespeare's plot. Having made Isabella sleep with Angelo, Marowitz's next step is perhaps inevitable: Angelo breaks his word to Isabella and as she leaves his bed she uncovers the severed head of her brother on his desk. We are prepared for the ensuing cover-up by a newly constructed scenes between Angelo and the Bishop. 'He who the sword of heaven will bear' is delivered as a rebuke, but, in contrast to his earlier treatment of Isabella, the Bishop benignly forgives Angelo. As the depths of the establishment's duplicity become apparent, Lucio is reintroduced as a choric observer of the action.

For the finale we return to the traditional presentation of the opening, although Isabella's accusations against Angelo are now truthful accounts of his behaviour rather than elements in an intrigue to trap him. A shortened version of the last scene continues up to the climax in Isabella's denunciation:

> But the next morn betimes,
> His purpose surfeiting, he sends a warrant
> For my poor brother's head.

There is 'a goodly pause' as the Duke surveys his comrades and for a moment there is tension as his next words – 'By heaven fond wretch' – appear to be addressed to Angelo. But ranks are closed and the play continues in restructured form to present a grim picture of society's leaders crushing an accuser. What was in Shakespeare an ironical denunciation of Angelo's behaviour becomes a brazen piece of whitewash:

By heaven fond wretch, thou knowest not what thou speak'st.
Or else thou art suborned against his honour
In hateful practice. First, his integrity
Stands without blemish. Next, it imports no reason
That with such vehemency he should pursue
Faults proper to himself. If he had so offended,
He would have weighed thy brother by himself,
And not have cut him off. Someone hath set you on.

The Duke now brings the full rigour of the law to silence
Isabella and Lucio. To create a ruthless exhibition of legal
violence Marowitz combines the more bitterly ironical of the
returned Duke's denunciations of Angelo's accusers with the
most ringing of Angelo's pronouncements on the law.

Thou foolish knave, and thou pernicious woman,
Think'st thou thy oaths,
Though they would swear down each particular saint,
Were testimonies against his worth and credit
That's sealed in approbation?
Thy slanders now shall by our laws be weighed
And by their justice priz'd. Take her to prison
And see our pleasure herein executed. To prison with her!
(*Turning front*) And all about that can hear, now hear this:
The law hath not been dead, though it hath slept.
Those many had not dared to do that evil
If that the first that did th'edict infringe
Had answered for his deed. Now 'tis awake,
Takes note of what is done, and like a prophet
Looks in a glass that shows what future evils,
Either now, or by remissness new, conceived,
Are now to have no successive degrees,
But 'ere they live, to end.

Like the 'measure for measure' speech by Shakespeare's Duke
this represents the last speech to the condemned person. But,
whereas in Shakespeare the speech completed an involved
jigsaw of intrigue to trap Angelo and test Isabella, Marowitz's
speech is delivered by a man who knows that Angelo is corrupt
and that Isabella is a victim of an evil system. As a final turn of
the screw, as Isabella is led away, Angelo takes her arm and

whispers what in Shakespeare is the Duke's proposal of marriage:

> I have a motion much imports your good,
> Whereto if you'll a willing ear incline,
> What's mine is yours, and what is yours is mine.

By now Isabella has nothing to learn about the moral degradation of her society. 'Expressionlessly shoving away Angelo's hand, she turns and moves off swiftly.'

In a witty coda the judges put aside their legal clothes and at a table piled with food and drink, ridicule their subjects and guffaw at the travesty of justice they have just perpetrated. Part of the exchanges concerning Lucio and Kate Keepdown are transformed into a mockingly ironical old lag's confession by Angelo (in a 'funny' working-class accent) to his fellow judges:

ANGELO If you will hang me for it, you may.
    But I had rather it would please you I might be whipped.
    (*All fall about with laughter*)
DUKE Whipped first, sir, and hanged after. (*This tops the last joke and all explode with even greater laughter*).
    Proclaim it, Provost, round about the city,
    If any woman wronged by this lewd fellow,
    As I have heard him swear himself there's one
    Whom he begot with child – let her appear,
    And he shall marry her.
ANGELO (*acting craven*). I beseech your highness, do not marry me to
    a whore. Marrying a punk, my Lord, is pressing to death,
    whipping *and* hanging.
DUKE (*pouring wine over* ANGELO's *head*). Slandering a prince deserves
    it.

After the savage farce of the formal law-giving Marowitz takes us behind the theatrical trappings of the law to show us his pillars of society as a group of 'Hurray Henries' brutishly laughing at their wickedness whilst guzzling food and drink.

15   WHAT THE PRODUCTIONS LOOKED LIKE: THE DESIGNERS'
VIEW

Like several Shakespeare comedies, *Measure for Measure* has
frequently been performed in historical or geographical
locations far from the Vienna (or London) of the early
seventeenth century. In 1975 there were two productions which
picked up the suggestive notion of setting a play involving
sexual repression in Vienna. Robin Phillips at Stratford,
Ontario, placed it before the First World War in the city of
Mahler and Arthur Schnitzler; Jonathan Miller at the
Greenwich Theatre, London, set it a quarter of a century later
in a Freudian Vienna with serial music. More recently, in 1981
a National Theatre production by Michael Rudman was set on
a post-colonial Caribbean island, with a lethargic ruler, a
clerical Angelo, some street-wise shanty-town dwellers, and a
few white officials such as Escalus and the Provost 'staying on'.
     None of the main productions moved very far from the early
seventeenth century, though the costumes for Kyle seemed
inspired by different parts of the century, the Duke wearing
a Jacobean gentleman's suit, Angelo and his officers
Commonwealth Puritan clothes. Barton brought some
Victorian touches to his comic characters, but basically none of
the four directors sought 'relevance' by updating or shifting the
locale.

The BBC production

This made the greatest efforts to achieve historical
authenticity, reflecting Cedric Messina's wish to give the
productions substance, but, unlike other early BBC
Shakespeare productions, the characters seemed to be wearing
clothes rather than stage robes out of the wardrobe. The
costume-designer Odette Barrow gave the clothes an Italian
look, arguing that it was 'quite possible' there was an influence
in early seventeenth-century Vienna. This was the only
production which did not imply that the city in Shakespeare's

mind was London. But the BBC designs gave a few nice insights into character: Vincentio wore gloves on all his ducal appearances, suggesting that he was protecting himself from contact with other people.

In designing the production Desmond Davis and Stuart Walker were seeking to create familiar points of reference for their audience. Davis took on features which it was hoped would be familiar to viewers from film conventions rather than from history or other stage productions. The prison sequence was played in winding corridors by the light of *flambeaux*, with dwarf gaolers shambling along as in a B-picture thriller. The brothel of I ii was even more familiar as the traditional Western saloon, with Mistress Overdone entering on an upper balcony smoking a cheroot and observing how business was progressing at the gambling-tables below.

Claustrophobic elements in the RSC and BBC designs

Many directors have detected in the play a closed world which they have tried to suggest in visual terms. The Actors' Touring Company production draped a loose rope around the acting area and removed it before the revelations and resolutions of the finale. Christopher Morley for Kyle and Timothy O'Brien for Barton designed settings which enclosed the characters within movable walls. O'Brien in 1970 designed a clinical set made up of cubes over a parquet flooring, a Scandinavian austerity matched by the symmetrical furniture of Angelo's rooms. For Kyle, Christopher Morley constructed a black box with numerous points of exit and entrance suggesting in the first scene a warren of corridors and offices. The box flattened out along the back of the stage to create barn-like cubicles where the whores copulated and which also served as prison cells. In both productions the walls swung inwards to enclose Angelo and Isabella for their intense second interview, and in 1978 an overhead spotlight picked out Angelo as he began to weaken in his first soliloquy.

These theatrical approaches were not open to the TV designers, but something similar was achieved by lighting. Their Vienna was 'a very dark, sinful city where no light got in'

(Davis in introduction to BBC edition), and many scenes were played at night, or at sunset or dawn, with the mist still clinging to the streets. This worked well in the long prison sequence, when tension was created whilst awaiting Angelo's instructions on Claudio. It was less effective when it militated against the realism which television imposed on the drama. The exposure of Claudio was a televisual *tour de force* with the camera rapidly tracking round the studio to give the impression that the prisoner was being dragged along endless streets. In practice one was left wondering why Angelo had chosen to shame the first transgressor of his regime in the middle of the night.

The most effective scenes in television terms were those which were shot most simply. Angelo in power was a superficially imposing figure, sitting at a large desk in front of the throne with armorial bearings. Camera angles made Angelo appear large behind the bureaucratic trappings of power; Isabella was a tiny figure huddled up in one corner. Only when Angelo became committed to what she was saying did the characters move closer into a single camera shot as their relationship became less public, more intimate.

Treatment of the last scene

Davis, Kyle and Marowitz wished to contrast the finale with the visual presentation of the earlier part of the play. For Kyle the black box was hidden and the scene was played on a white carpet on the forestage. Marowitz's Duke returned to Vienna wearing imposing gold trimmings on his clothes, but, once formal business was over, the judges took off their gowns to reveal bright casual clothes beneath. The play ended with an exposed view of these cruel men, their theatrical accoutrements laid aside. Davis emphasised that the finale was the last part of an intrigue in which the Duke, Isabella and Mariana were play-acting. For the first time a scene was played in sunshine, which revealed the truth. To suggest the theatricalism of the scene it was set on raised scaffolding, with something of the structure of a Jacobean stage, on which the Duke, Isabella, Angelo and Mariana acted out the final moments of their plot before the gaze of the Viennese citizenry. This idea of watching, of Vienna being a city where behaviour was public property, was taken further by Barry Kyle. In the second scene, sexual activity took place in public; the whores watched much of the action from their cells at the back of the stage, and they stared down at Angelo from the gallery before his public shaming in the finale. In the Caribbean *Measure for Measure* Angelo received the most public exposure of all, the Duke having made his entry into the city through what appeared to be its most squalid, crowded quarter. Economic necessity had turned Barton's *Measure for Measure* into something of a chamber production, and the lack of supernumeraries in the finale meant that the characters were being morally weighed for each other's benefit rather than as a public spectacle.

Physical contrast between the two regimes

Both Barton and Kyle sought to make a design contrast between the easy-going regime of the Duke and the forceful one of Angelo. In 1970 the harshness of the set was softened in the first scene by untidy piles of books lying on the table. The Duke smoked his pipe in his scholar's cap to the gentle sound of a chiming clock outside. When he left he pressed a large book into Angelo's hands, who disdainfully brushed away the dust from the seldom-used volume. Once he was established in power, the books disapppeared and only basic, utilitarian writing-materials – parchment, quills, ink pot, sand pot – were visible. Angelo's clean sweep extended literally to his rooms.

Barry Kyle and Christopher Morley took the contrast even further. When installing Angelo in office the Duke placed a judicial robe on him, a white garment slashed with red tongues of fire. This became a symbol of Angelo's regime: his judges carried the motif on their robes, all the victims of the newly invoked laws were obliged to wear similar garments in prison. Taking Isabella's famous lines about 'man, proud man/ Dressed in a little brief authority' as a starting-point, Kyle made clothes, especially uniforms, a feature which bound the production together. Once in his gown, Angelo became addicted to the exercise of power; when Pompey crossed the boundary between law-breaker and law-enforcer he outdid his snooty superior Abhorson by investing himself in a splendid leather headsman's uniform. In contrast, the victims of these proudly uniformed men and women were stripped to their underwear, and Barnadine, the law's ultimate long-term prisoner, appeared (in earlier performances) stark naked. As a counter-movement, the Duke seemed to draw the confidence of wisdom from his friar's clothes, and even after his exposure in the finale he continued to wear them loosely draped over his tunic and breeches.

Legal symbols in the Marowitz and Kyle productions

Properties (or the lack of them) were used by Barton and Davis to give an insight into Angelo's character and the nature of his society. Robin Don, the designer of the Marowitz production, also employed a few telling symbols to convey the world of the play. The audience at the Open Space Theatre were seated in what was variously described as jury boxes or church pews, the traditional places for passing moral judgements on one's fellow men. The Duke's throne was impressively upholstered in red, but the arm concealed a secret drinks compartment. At the back of the stage hung a large parchment setting out the law against sexual immorality. When Isabella gave herself to Angelo, the parchment was flown up to reveal a bed bathed in red light where they were to make love – a symbol, as the *Guardian* critic remarked (29 May 1975), of 'the law corrupting itself behind the shelter of its own legality.'

Legal symbols also played an important part in Kyle's production, the sword of justice in particular being prominently on view from the start. Angelo hesitantly examined it during his words to Escalus at the end of the first scene, but once secure in his robes and his authority he sat confidently with the sword across his knees for the interrogation of Pompey. Once Angelo had left the room, Escalus casually leaned the sword against the table for his more relaxed administration of justice. With Pompey departed, Escalus and the Justice removed their gowns to talk, man to man, with their junior legal executive Elbow. As in Marowitz the judges remove their theatrical robes to act as men; the contrast, however, could not be more striking, Escalus and his fellow appearing as tolerant, kindly human beings once divested of their formal garments.

16 WOMEN AND SAINTS: THE ISABELLAS

Isabellas can be characterised by the nature of their defence of chastity. No modern audience could accept an Isabella like Sarah Siddons, whose denunciations of vice, it was said, made Georgian rakes go weak at the knees. But by the end of the 1970s it was possible to tolerate an Isabella who stoutly defended her honour from the best of feminist motives. We could suggest a range of modern responses to Isabella's dilemma which range from 'She is wrong and should be condemned', through 'She is wrong but we should sympathise', to 'She is right, why should she if she doesn't want to?' There have been productions in the last quarter of a century which have taken the 'tough' line on Isabella – Bond characterised her for Keith Hack as a 'vicious sex hysteric' – but broadly speaking the Isabellas of Estelle Kohler (1970), Paola Dionisotti (1978), and Kate Nelligan (1979) provoked 'softer' responses.

Ciaran Madden (Open Space, 1975)

For Ciaran Madden of course the problem did not arise in the standard form: her Isabella took the conscious decision to sleep with Angelo in hope of an exchange for her brother. Marowitz was asking his actress for a human, essentially innocent victim of corruption. As he puts it, his Isabella is 'human rather than angelic and her dilemma is one that connects with human conflicts and demands human solutions' (*Plays and Players,* June 1975). Ciaran Madden had already played Isabella two years earlier in a conventional production at the Yvonne Arnaud Theatre, but to Marowitz's less complex characterisation she brought many appropriate qualities. She had a fresh, healthy type of beauty, perfectly capable of getting under the guard of any Puritan. Robert Cushman in the *Observer* (15 June 1975) praised Miss Madden in the role as an actress who 'does not circle her emotions or tunnel underneath them' but confronted them head on. She was particularly powerful in her rage at Claudio, her feelings founded on the unworldly confidence of a convent girl. When she discovered the nature of society's leaders she registered only waxen astonishment as she was led away to prison. In only one respect was it felt she left out part of her character, and that was the element of base sensuality which Marowitz emphasises. Although Miss Madden appeared to leave Angelo's bed not dissatisfied by the experience, in general her performance did not exude the coarse yearning for immorality which Marowitz lays bare in the central collage section.

Like all four Isabellas, Ciaran Madden wore the traditional nun's white habit, and, although it has become something of a stage tradition to do so, it has not always been followed. In 1908 William Poel pointed out that Isabella was only a novice and was not entitled to wear the robes. Poel's Isabella – the appropriately named Sara Allgood – wore the conventional clothes of a Jacobean lady. More recently Judi Dench in the 1962 RSC production did not dress as a nun. Today, whatever the authentic liturgical position, an Isabella in the vestments of the nunnery is too potent an image for most directors to do without. For Barry Kyle, Isabella's habit was another example of the exterior authority in which the characters wrap themselves.

Estelle Kohler (Stratford, 1970)

In John Barton's production Estelle Kohler was an exceptionally youthful figure, pretty rather than attractive in a way that this Angelo would find lust-provoking. She was far from being a frail victim; her standards were proclaimed with a ringing declaration of intent. On the touchstone line 'More than our brother is our chastity' [II iv 185], she 'flings out her arm in an imperious gesture like a flamboyant general leading the troops to battle' (Harold Hobson, *The Sunday Times*, 5 April

1970). This Isabella was a moral show-off hiding her uncertainties about sexuality beneath an heroic protection of her virginity which bordered on the melodramatic. When she knelt to Angelo at their first meeting it seemed as though she was to embrace him before the gesture turned into a pleading one. Miss Kohler's Isabella was a powerful advocate, an independent young lady who manoeuvred herself into the position of strength behind Angelo's desk. Uncertain as to the nature of her feelings, she seemed to find a masochistic comfort in each rejection, which prompted her to heights of rage against the injustice of society and the presumption of mankind. It was also, some critics found, a rage against the male sex ('Man, proud *man*' was the emphasis), and D. A. N. Jones (*Listener*, 9 April 1970) argued strongly for a feminist element in Miss Kohler's performance with her chastity a symbol of her integrity. With her brother her immaturity was more apparent: when it seemed as though he were prepared to die, she registered intense relief and sat down on the bench by his side; as he weakened she broke down in silent tears until mounting resentment took brother and sister to opposite ends of the prison table. The Duke was obliged to come between them as if they were naughty children in the nursery; characteristically, a moment later they were back in each other's arms.

But it was the independence of Isabella which was most relevant for the controversial ending of Barton's production: Isabella's reaction to the Duke's second proposal of marriage. (Isabella had fainted when Claudio appeared and was too overcome to pay any attention to the first proposal.) Although this production is often described as 'the one in which Isabella rejected the Duke', Barton has always denied that he intended any simple interpretation. 'What I actually intended', he has said, 'was that Isabella's response should be open-ended . . . . The last thing that I presented on stage . . . was Isabella wondering, puzzling about what she should do' (interview with Gareth Lloyd Evans in *Aspects of Shakespeare's 'Problem Plays'*). However, the director's rational statement of intention after the event did not always tally with what members of the audience saw in the theatre. In a perceptive review in the *Sunday Telegraph* (5 April 1970) Frank Marcus felt that the final impact of Isabella left alone on stage suggested that she was now

'suddenly aware that she contained within her body a force so
irresistible that Justice, Piety, Loyalty, Charity, and ...
Majesty are powerless before it'. For D. A. N. Jones pursuing
his feminist critique, Isabella glared out at the audience 'silent
rage written all over her high forehead and stubborn chin',
furious that again she was being treated as a chattel, this time
by the presumptuous Duke. Such diverse reaction to the end of
the production suggests that the moment was a highly charged
one. Crucially for the story of *Measure for Measure* on the stage,
Barton had opened up a theatrical problem which directors
and actresses would have to address. Whether Isabellas reject
their Dukes, or enthusiastically accept them, an audience must
expect to find an explanation in the earlier scenes of the play.

Kate Nelligan (BBC, 1979)

This was a challenge which Paola Dionisotti's Isabella took up
but Kate Nelligan's was unable to accept. At the end of Davis's
Measure for Measure Miss Nelligan paused for a few seconds to
consider her decision, smiled, and indicated her acceptance.
Nothing in her earlier scenes explained her reasons for this
decision and we were left to wonder whether she was motivated
by passionate love for the Duke, a desire to become Duchess of
Vienna, or a rejection of the values of the convent. The problem
was more acute in Miss Nelligan's case as, of all four Isabellas,
she seemed most suited to the cloistered life, her glacial beauty
never suggesting for one moment the touches of sensuality or
feminine stubbornness which other actresses discovered in the
role. Kate Nelligan's performance was an honest attempt to
take Isabella on her own evaluation as a passionate believer in
the doctrine that 'moral good and evil are forces which people
will lay down their lives for' (Miss Nelligan in the Introduction
to the BBC edition). This after all is what Isabella says she is
prepared to do, and Miss Nelligan had no time for charges of
hypocrisy, dogmatism or sexual neurosis. Isabella believed in a
commitment to chastity and Angelo's ruthless pursuit put an
intolerable strain on her but, in Miss Nelligan's words, she is 'a
good woman in any sense of the word'. This dedication to
morality was the motive power behind the scenes with Angelo,

but by the second half of the production all the old objections to Isabella's behaviour had resurfaced. If she is attracted to honesty, why does she allow herself to be drawn into a plot which will involve deceit? And why does she marry the Duke rather than return to the Order of which she would seem such a suitable member? It was a refreshing essay at a plain performance, but one cannot now return to the pre-1970 Isabella who can be accepted on her own terms and who will leave the stage at the end smiling on the arm of the Duke.

Paola Dionisotti (Stratford, 1978)

If Kate Nelligan seemed the likeliest candidate for the nunnery, Paola Dionisotti always appeared an unlikely one, even though she made her first entrance carrying what seemed to be her entire worldly possessions. Miss Dionisotti's performance was not greatly liked by the critics and there was a general feeling that she was miscast. One critic ungallantly wondered how anyone could desire 'so mousy, dowdy and unattractive a figure' (*Warwick Advertiser*, 20 June). There was little physical similarity to the Isabellas of Madden, Nelligan and Kohler, but out of an unprepossessing exterior Miss Dionisotti created an interesting flesh-and-blood heroine whose increasing self-awareness was a counterpoint to Michael Pennington's Duke. The two scenes usually considered actor-proof, the interviews with Angelo, were least successful, in part because they lacked any erotic charge. But Miss Dionisotti came into her own in the later stages of the play as her relationship with the Duke developed. If in fact this was a production about 'people waking up to their true natures' as Michael Billington wrote in the *Guardian* (28 June), this Isabella's goal was the realisation of the warm-blooded woman hidden beneath her habit. At times her femininity broke out in moments of petulant anger, impotently kicking a pile of prisoners' clothes, or wild despair, tearing off her veil and rosary on hearing that her brother was dead. She was drawn to the Duke by his newly discovered confidence and charm and by their mutual excitement in the plan to trap Angelo. In the pleasure she got from the intrigue Miss Dionisotti became an engaging heroine, giggling as she mapped out with straw the scene of Mariana's assignation in Angelo's garden. When the Duke eventually proposed marriage her reaction was so enthusiastic that his second proposal was cut from the text, and his response 'But fitter time for that' [v i 490] to this passionate young woman carried the knowing smile which suggested a cooling-off period before enthusiastic love-making.

17   Bureaucrats and Devils: The Angelos

We might classify our Angelos, in rough and ready shorthand, by the depth of their evil, by how far they retained our residual sympathy. A suggestion twenty-five years ago that Angelo was anything but a black-hearted villain would have been treated with derision, but recent productions have presented Angelos as men whose behaviour derives from their weakness or immaturity. Ian Richardson (1970) and Jonathan Pryce (1978) were flawed personalities, albeit, in Richardson's case, capable of great brutality. Tim Piggott-Smith (1979) occupied a neutral position.

Nikolas Simmonds (Open Space, 1975)

Through the nature of the adaptation, Simmonds's Angelo was a more depraved character than in Shakespeare's text. Catherine Itzin described him as 'malevolent as the snake . . . slow, quiet, eyes hooded, as dangerous as a viper' (*Plays and Players*, July 1975). To find uncomplicated evil like this we have to go back through John Gielgud's Angelo in 1950 – 'sinister so far as a real man can be sinister' (H. G. Mathews, *Theatre World*) – to Charles Laughton in 1933, whom Tyrone Guthrie remembered as 'a cunning, oleaginous monster whose cruelty and lubricity could have surprised no one, least of all himself' (*A Life in the Theatre*). In addition to this, Simmonds's Angelo, one should remember, took Isabella's virginity, had her brother beheaded, and walked away scot-free and laughing at the end. It is possible that Marowitz's Angelo was in part reaction to the tolerant, liberalising assessments which directors had recently put on stage.

Ian Richardson (Stratford, 1970)

Richardson's Angelo was the most generally acclaimed feature of this production. Although physically beautiful, he was a fallen angel, proud, arrogant, rigid and ice-cold in principle. The *Morning Star* critic pointed out that Richardson was 'a sinister, repressed chorister', and indeed his cruelty and coarseness seemed to proceed from the immaturity of an adolescent. When he had finally made his intentions clear to Isabella, Richardon knelt before her, but he seized her angrily after her waspish response and butted her across the room onto his table, where he roughly caressed her body. The crude savagery of his attack seemed unnecessarily explicit to some observers, but Richardson's immature sexuality could only express itself in this brutal, unsophisticated way. Some critics also saw that his sadism seemed to be unleashed by a complementary masochism in Estelle Kohler's Isabella. One of the most powerful moments in Richardson's performance was his soliloquy in IV iv. Barton strengthened the scene by providing an appearance for the Provost here. Following instructions, he carried a basket containing, Angelo supposed, Claudio's head. Confronted with this physical reminder of what he had done, Richardson broke down and wept like a child at his desk. Despite his pride and cruelty, Richardson's Angelo, because of its childishness, inspired a good deal of pathos. For Frank Marcus he was the little man whose only source of sexual satisfaction is to fondle girls on crowded underground trains. This lack of evil grandeur, the essential pettiness of Richardson's cruelty, meant that his release from adult punishment did not seem inappropriate.

Tim Piggott-Smith (BBC, 1979)

Like his Isabella, Tim Piggott-Smith tried to give a

straightforward   performance,   uncluttered   by   much
psychological underpinning. This was an Angelo who had been
waiting for power, seeking it for its own sake as well as for the
opportunity of enforcing his principles. He seemed at first a
commanding figure who might do great things compared to the
uncertain, nervous Duke. He was efficient and businesslike
when we saw him at his great table and, like many Angelos, he
was dealing with documents when Isabella entered. Ian
Richardson had curtly snapped, 'Y'are welcome' before
looking up from his work to take in his visitor. Piggott-Smith
seemed unmoved by Kate Nelligan until well into the scene, up
to the point when she asks him to look for sexual feelings within
himself. He was an arrogant, unattractive man, but emotions
were there, buried beneath a busy façade of paperwork and
official routine. Once the explosion of his passion was over, he
was lost, unable to reshape his life into its old reliable paths.

Jonathan Pryce (Stratford, 1978)

Jonathan Pryce was such a pathetic figure that some critics
wondered if the moral balance of the play had been overturned.
If Piggott-Smith had been waiting for his opportunity to turn
Vienna his way, Pryce seemed ill at ease at the prospect of
power. The series of cues in the first scene in which the Duke
seems to be offering some symbol of authority to Angelo were
opened out by Kyle to suggest the deputy's agitation and
doubt. At 'Hold therefore, Angelo' [i i 42]the Duke held out a
cloak of justice, but Angelo backed away up stage, only
accepting it ten lines later on 'Take your honours' [52]. If Tim
Piggott-Smith's Angelo seemed like a senior official in the
Viennese court who might reasonably expect temporary
power, Jonathan Pryce looked like a minor figure in the
hierarchy, a shy theorist with little knowledge or liking for
human problems. His hands were constantly on the move, he
plaited his fingers together as if, Michael Billington
commented, 'they were copulating stick-insects'. Like
Richardson, Pryce had a distaste for dust, though in his case the
specks seemed imaginary. All his fidgety gestures expressed
deep sexual frustration. Only when installed in power with his

robes and his sword did he gain confidence, and in misusing his authority to pressurise Isabella he achieved authority. The callow youth turned to old-fashioned moral legalism to clean up his city. When his position presented him with a chance to satisfy his suppressed lust, he gleefully seized the opportunity whilst being overcome with disgust at this outburst of unseemly feeling. The long, roundabout route to his final blunt proposition reflected this conflict between lust and self-loathing and at climactic moments Pryce turned away from the seated Isabella to address his remarks to the enclosing walls, ashamed to meet her hostile gaze. When in the finale it became obvious that his fate was sealed, Pryce withdrew into a catatonic state, staring vacantly ahead of him, terrified, in the words of the *Daily Mail* reviewer (28 June 1978), of 'the devils that he sees lurking over his shoulder'. Like Isabella and the Duke, Angelo had come to realise his true nature, but unlike his opponents, self-knowledge had brought torment and despair.

18   PROFESSIONAL PEOPLE AND VAUDEVILLE TURNS: THE
BROTHEL AND PRISON SCENES

For a completely satisfactory *Measure for Measure* an effective presentation of the wider world of Vienna is vital. We need some impression of the people the Duke is so anxious to avoid and who provide the material whose messy lives Angelo strives to control.

   In cutting out the sub-plot Marowitz was concentrating attention on the moral and social questions of the story. As we have seen earlier, these sections were always cut before the nineteenth century, and even today Marowitz is not the only director who has jettisoned the lower depths in the interests of bolstering up the allegedly more serious bits of the play. A production by the Tavistock Repertory Theatre Company at the Tower Theatre, London, in 1972 cut out the underworld in the belief that attempts to enliven these scenes 'degenerate into exercises in linguistic archaeology'. One curious aspect of Marowitz's adaptation is that he retained Lucio in the earlier

'Shakespearean' portion and reintroduced him later as a sardonic commentator. But a Lucio cut adrift from his seedy environment seemed superfluous, particularly as Marowitz was showing with admirable clarity the corruption which Lucio was describing. Claudio on the other hand remained as a striking contrast to Isabella, Brian Gwaspari's whinging adolescent provoking the towering rage of his sister.

Stratford, 1970

It was generally agreed that the treatment of Viennese low life in Barton's production was weak, something which led some critics to describe the total effect of the production as over-cerebral, untheatrical, or thin-blooded. There was so little sign of the baser animal instincts that Benedict Nightingale in the *New Statesman* commented (10 April 1978) that 'rarely can so sensual a play have been knocked so senseless'. Unusually for Barton, the characters in this part of the play, with the exception of Terrence Hardiman's Lucio, failed to be realised as human beings. Pompey (John Kane) had one lively moment when he tore down Angelo's proclamation against the brothels, but thereafter he joined a company of vaudeville grotesques whose comic routines seemed embarrassingly unfunny.

The prison in which these amiable cards ended up, with its scrubbed wooden tables and chorus of singing prisoners, seemed a tolerable place to spend some time, and for its most celebrated occupant, Barnadine, Barton went for the easy option, a heavily bearded tosspot, like a long-term prisoner out of *The Count of Monte Cristo*. (Despite his nakedness, Kyle's Barnadine, Conrad Asquith, remained dignified and unbowed by his years in the condemned cell.) The 1970 Barnadine (David Waller or Anthony Langdon) staggered up through a trap-door to urinate into a chamber-pot which later received the Friar's proffered crucifix. This childish piece of sacrilege was of a piece with the touches of Victoriana in these scenes: Pompey did a music-hall turn, playing the spoons for his fellow prisoners, and Abhorson (Ted Valentine) looked like a cross between a seaside bather and Sweeney Todd with his coiffeured hairstyle, his Bible, and his intoning of 'Man that is born of woman' to the indifferent Barnadine. By such irrelevancies the production made light of the unregenerate elements in *Measure for Measure*; these scamps and cartoon characters were no more part of the general corruption that was overwhelming Vienna than they were flesh-and-blood characters demanding toleration or condemnation.

The saving grace of this part of the play was Terrence Hardiman's rat-like Lucio. Like his concept of Toby Belch in the previous season's *Twelfth Night* or the Falstaff of his *Henry IV*, Barton introduced his principal comic character as a superficially engaging figure. But as the action progressed layers of character were stripped away to reveal shallow viciousness beneath the *savoir faire* and conviviality. This interpretation follows the broad lines of Shakespeare's play, where Lucio is at first at his best trying to save Claudio and chivvying Isabella along in her appeals to Angelo. In the nunnery he stationed himself in front of a religious statue whilst describing the sensual love of Claudio and Juliet. But by the later prison scenes, with the teasing of Pompey and the slandering of the Duke – Hardiman threw a coin to the Friar on 'I prithee pray for me' [III ii 170] – it was clear that Lucio's wit and comic intelligence were negative and deflating rather than life-enhancing. For once his punishment, which he received with supremely arrogant insouciance, seemed justified.

BBC production, 1979

John McEnery for Davis remained a sympathetic Lucio throughout, retaining a lingering fondness for Isabella to the end. The brothel and prison scenes were, we have seen, presented in strong, visual terms and Frank Middlemass made Pompey at once grotesque and a proud professional man. Although Adrienne Corri's glamorous Mistress Overdone avoided the pantomime-dame treatment of some other productions, the whores on TV, and to some extent in all the productions, tended to revert to type as the raddled, Cockneyfied harridans of stage convention.

Stratford, 1978

Barry Kyle's treatment of these scenes was masterly in concept and execution. By showing in detail the effect of Angelo on the lower orders in the front line of his moral attack, we were made aware of the deadening lethargy of the previous regime and of the energy which Angelo brought to bear on it. The cubicles for copulation, far removed from any fantasy brothel, and Richard Griffith's Pompey dutifully going about his work in an undemonstrative way suggested that even sexual excitement was flagging in the Duke's Vienna. Similarly, the Provost dragged out of storage and dusted down the execution block not used for twenty years. The change of pace associated with Angelo was reflected in the steady stream of new arrivals in this businesslike prison, each convict being carefully booked in, stripped, issued with a standard uniform and assigned a cell, whilst Constable Elbow was handed a note of further disreputables for rounding up.

   That a kind of justice could still be administered under an Angelo was made clear in the interrogation of Froth and Pompey, the only scene in these productions which produced genuine laughter. Richard Griffiths as Pompey had obviously been in this situation many times before and had no difficulty in talking his way out of trouble. Geoffrey Freshwater's Elbow was the traditional bone-headed Mr Plod with his notebook and whistle, which, to the consternation of all on stage, he blew lustily at the outrageous suggestion that he premaritally 'respected' his wife. He was clearly out of his depth in following what was going on and it was a very, very long time before it became clear to him that Pompey was going to walk out of court unpunished. Froth was so overjoyed by being let off with a warning that he presented Escalus and the Justice with little flowers which they accepted with good grace and carefully attached to their clothes. These details created the impression of a human scale of behaviour once Angelo was out of the way. Once Pompey and Froth had left and gowns were doffed, Elbow was eager to submit himself to the instructions of his betters: 'To your worship's house, sir?' [II i 261] was delivered in the hushed, awed tones of the archetypal 'gaffer's man'.

19   MEN NOT GODS: THE DUKES

At the beginning of the 1970s the character of the Duke was carrying an overload of symbolism which by the end of the decade it had shed. Having passed through a period when the Duke was the principal villain in a dark, bitter view of the play – most notably in Richard Mayes's unctuous performance for Marowitz – he ended the decade with a weight of psychological motives to explain his eccentric behaviour. Not all actors have taken this intense view of the character. Bernard Lloyd in a Birmingham Repertory Theatre production in 1976 was a merry prankster who could hardly wait to get away from Vienna to begin his japes. But this lightweight performance was something of a reaction to the general seriousness of purpose with which the Dukes have set about their activities.

Kenneth Colley (BBC, 1979)

It is generally agreed that Sebastian Shaw's all-too-human Duke for Barton turned the play away from the path of allegorical Dukes and deistic symbolism. As a result some sort of viewpoint was expected of a director to account for the oddities of the Duke's personality. Kenneth Colley was the exception to this pattern. Colley certainly created a rounded character out of some of the elements in the role. On his first entrance he passed hurriedly down his audience chamber to the polite applause of his courtiers, showing obvious signs of unease at this exposure to popular acclaim whilst at the same time trying to retain some ducal dignity. Once he had adopted a friar's role he went about his task with sincerity and urgency; he seemed desperately anxious to instil in Claudio the disdain for life which would take him to the block with some composure, and was similarly concerned to comfort Isabella with a fraternal hug when she was told that Claudio was dead. But when this nicely conceived character gets involved in the intrigue of the later part of the play we are merely left with a tangle of inconsistencies. If Colley's Duke was such a benevolent figure why did he let Isabella suffer so long? What are we to make of his religious piety in the light of his later actions? Without some dimly perceived motive at its heart, the Duke's character will no longer hold together.

Sebastian Shaw (RSC, 1970)

In a seminal programme note for her husband's production, Anne Barton pointed out that, if the Duke is 'an image of Providence, there would seem to be chaos in Heaven'. This was the starting-point for Sebastian Shaw's fumbling, smiling Duke, endlessly trying, and failing, to manipulate lives which he had confused in the first place. He was a man in late middle age, amiable, capable of inspiring a dogged affection, but an incompetent and ultimately dangerous ruler. From the smirks and astonished giggles which greeted the mention of Angelo, the Duke's assessment of his capability seemed to be his own. Closeted too long amongst books, Shaw's judgement of men was severely warped, and, aware of this, he felt obliged to scurry about to try and sort out the confusions arising from the transfer of power. His performance was constructed around a series of rejections, as his offers were ignored or rejected. Juliet interrupts him to bring his moralising to an end; Claudio is more interested in his dinner than a speech on the vanity of life; Barnadine brushes him aside and desecrates his crucifix. To all these rebuffs Shaw smiled abstractedly and dithered off to try and help elsewhere. He remained a likable figure, sharing a drink with Lucio and not over-concerned by the portrait of his alleged weaknesses. We saw briefly the respect he was capable of inspiring. When the Provost raised difficulties about tricking Angelo, Shaw held up a lantern in the darkening prison on 'You know the character, I doubt not' [iv ii 187–8]. The Provost fell to his knees and kissed his hand.

Despite a residual trace of authority, however, Shaw's Duke was a pathetic figure, a lonely, aging man whose routine recital of life's pains was suddenly charged with personal relevance when he came to the sorrows of old age:

> when thou art old and rich,
> Thou has neither heat, affection, limb, nor beauty
> To make thy riches pleasant. What's yet in this
> That bears the name of life? [III i 36–9]

His fear of a loveless old age made the final moments of the play particularly painful, though Shaw himself was briskly unsympathetic to the Duke's plan to marry Isabella: he was 'a stupid man' to believe that a young girl would fall into his arms (interview with Terry Coleman, *Guardian*, 13 April 1970). In the course of their joint intrigue the Duke had indicated on several occasions his growing affection for Isabella: on 'Command these fretting waters from your eyes' [IV iii 146] he gave her an ambiguously warm kiss. The moment of truth was pitiable in the extreme: Shaw pushed himself between the ecstatically happy brother and sister to make his proposal of marriage. Isabella stared at him horror-struck and Escalus stepped forward to break the embarrassed silence with a tactful cough. Rubbing his spectacles, Shaw's 'So' (in the last line of the play) could just have carried the implication that at last he appreciated the impossibility of making people behave as you want them to simply because you have power. Shaw's final judgement on his character – 'a pitiful sadistic man getting what he deserves' – seemed over-harsh for the dejected, slightly more self-aware figure who left the stage.

Michael Pennington (RSC, 1978)

This Duke made a more rapid, certainly happier, journey to self-awareness. Unlike Shaw's complacent pipe-smoker, Pennington seemed ill at ease at his decision to leave Vienna in Angelo's hands, nervously twisting himself around the involved syntax of the first speech as he sought Escalus's approval for what he had done. The donning of the Friar's robes seemed to instil confidence in him, and he poured out the long speech to Claudio astonished at his newly acquired articulateness. With the alterations to the prison scenes noted earlier, Pennington was able to stand back and watch the wide-ranging effects of the transfer of power at grass-roots level.

Confident in his role and deeply affected by what he had seen, the Duke was able to draw on his knowledge of Angelo's previous history to unfold a plan of action to Isabella.

In the second half of the production Pennington could propel the play along with a lively, dynamic momentum. Physically youthful and good-looking, he established a natural rapport with Mariana, Isabella and the audience. With Mariana he relaxed on a hay stook with a bottle of wine, injecting a note of joy and fecundity into the desiccated world of the city. By the finale it was clear that the Duke was withholding news of Claudio's reprieve to see whether Isabella would respond with a Christian appeal for mercy. Wearing the Friar's robes in which he had learnt so much, Pennington delivered the 'measure for measure' speech with arms outstretched and in a voice sonorous with authority, his eyes never leaving Isabella's face. When she pleaded for Angelo's life, Claudio could be delivered from the prison and Isabella give herself to the Duke. Christian forgiveness, joyful sexuality, confident self-knowledge synthesised with a harmony which owed nothing to the mechanical tidying-up of romantic comedy, it had been achieved with such difficulty. It was a harmony, moreover, brought about by the experiences and self-analysis of the characters rather than an external scheme of divine providence imposed on the action from outside.

READING LIST

The New Penguin edition used in this book has a good introduction by Professor Nosworthy and there is a succinct bibliography. The Cambridge Shakespeare edition, edited by Sir Arthur Quiller Couch and John Dover Wilson, has also been consulted, as has the Arden Shakespeare edition (1965). This edition is the most convenient place to read the sources for *Measure for Measure*. The BBC also brought out an edition in 1979 in conjunction with Desmond Davis's production.

The Marowitz adaptation was first published in *Plays and Players*, June 1975, but it also appears in *The Marowitz Shakespeare* (1978) with other adaptations and collages and an introduction by Marowitz.

CRITICISM AND STAGE HISTORY

A good way into the bewildering critical history of *Measure for Measure* is to consult one of the recent critical anthologies of the play: *'Measure for Measure': A Casebook*, ed. C. K. Stead (1971); *Aspects of Shakespeare's 'Problem Plays': Articles Reprinted from 'Shakespeare Survey'*, ed. Kenneth Muir and Stanley Wells (1982).

The stage history of *Measure for Measure* has not been written and information has to be gleaned from several sources. Charles Odell, *Shakespeare from Betterton to Irving* (1921), and J. C. Trewin, *Shakespeare on the English Stage 1900–1964* (1964), carry the story to the terminal date of Trewin's book. There are a few reviews in both anthologies cited above and a short stage history in the Cambridge edition by Harold Child, though this is little more than a list of names and dates. In *Shakespeare Survey 1972* Herbert S. Weil's 'The Options of the Audience: Theory and Practice in Peter Brook's *Measure for Measure*' is an informative account of a seminal production. There have been three good studies of recent productions which I have found very helpful: Jane Williamson, 'The Duke and Isabella on the Modern Stage', in *The Triple Bond*, ed. Joseph G. Price (1975); Ralph Berry, *Changing Styles in Shakespeare* (1981); Michael Scott, '*Measure for Measure*', in *Renaissance Drama and a Modern Audience* (1982).

Reviews of the four main productions can be found in most national newspapers and journals for about a fortnight after their first nights. The student may well find that these ephemeral pieces contain some of the most incisive and enlivening criticism of the play.

INDEX OF NAMES